using the meta quest 3 in the workplace

An Insanely Simple Guide to the Meta Quest 3

scott la counte

contents

introduction

Unlocking the Potential of Meta Quest 3

The Meta Quest platform has earned its reputation as a gateway to virtual gaming adventures. Yet, beneath its entertainment veneer, lies potential that's waiting to be tapped into. The capabilities of this device aren't confined to the gaming world; they can seamlessly blend into our everyday professional lives. This guide offers you a deep dive into the often uncharted territories of the Meta Quest 3, highlighting its prowess not just as a gaming console, but as a tool that can redefine how we approach our work.

Inside, you'll explore:

- Setup & Basics: Step-by-step guidance to initiate your journey, ensuring you make the most out of your device from the get-go.

- Productivity Tools: An overview of tailored apps and programs specifically designed for the Quest 3, helping you manage tasks, engage in virtual meetings, and draft out creative projects.
- Virtual Workspaces: Techniques to curate your personalized virtual office, engage in global conferences, and present with a touch of flair.
- Maintenance & Care: A look into keeping your device in prime condition, ensuring it serves you well for years to come.
- Relax & Unwind: While work is essential, so is relaxation. Delve into some fun and calming recreational uses of the device after a productive day.

Beyond its gaming facade, the Meta Quest 3 harbors immense potential in transforming the professional realm. Whether you're an entrepreneur, a remote worker, or someone simply curious about how technology can reshape traditional work methodologies, this guide promises insights that are not just innovative but also practically implementable.

Step into a world where virtual reality merges with reality, changing our perception of work and collaboration.

1 /
start here

META QUEST 3 was like nothing I had seen before. From the moment I put it on my head, I saw the future in front of my eyes. There was a small problem, however. It's like nothing I had used before–not a lot about it was intuitive.

This book is to help people like me who are blow away by how amazing it is and want to make sure they understand just how to use it.

The focus of the book will be on productivity; it will touch on VR gaming and entertainment, but the purpose is to teach you how to use it for your everyday work to be more productive.

2 /
vr, mr, ar: breaking down the virtual alphabet soup

BEFORE WE GET to the heart of the book–the Meta Quest 3 and how to use it–I am going to take a step back and talk about what exactly it is, because there's a lot of misconceptions. True, the Quest 3 is a VR (virtual reality) headset–but it also does MR (mixed reality) and AR (augmented reality). But what does that mean exactly? Lets break it down!

vr: virtual reality

Imagine strapping on a headset, and within moments, finding yourself in an entirely different world – maybe under the ocean, atop a mountain, or even in outer space. This is VR in a nutshell

.

Core Features:

- Full Immersion: VR is all about immersing the user in a completely digital environment. Once you put on a VR headset, your surroundings transform entirely, and you become part of a new world.
- Interaction: Modern VR platforms often come with handheld controllers, allowing users to interact with the virtual environment – like grabbing objects, throwing them, or even drawing in mid-air.

Use Cases:

- Gaming: A significant draw to VR is the gaming industry. Games like "Beat Saber" and "Half-Life: Alyx" have showcased the potential of VR as an entertainment platform.
- Education: VR can transport students to ancient civilizations, inside the human body, or even to distant galaxies – making learning experiential.

- Training: From surgical practices to flight simulations, VR provides a risk-free environment to hone skills.

ar: augmented reality

Ever tried catching Pokémon in the real world using your smartphone? If so, you've experienced Augmented Reality (AR).

Core Features:

- Overlay of Digital Content: Unlike VR, which immerses you in a completely digital environment, AR overlays digital content onto the real world.
- See-through Experience: Most AR applications are through devices where you can still see the real world, like your smartphone or certain specialized glasses.
- Interactivity with the Real World: AR allows digital and real-world elements to interact in unique ways. For instance, you can see a virtual furniture piece in your actual living

room before making a purchase decision.

Use Cases:

- Gaming: Games like "Pokémon GO" leverage AR to merge fictional characters with real-world locations.
- Shopping: Retailers use AR apps to let users try on makeup, clothes, or see how furniture looks in their homes virtually.
- Navigation: Some AR applications can overlay directions onto the real world, making it easier for users to navigate unfamiliar places.

mr: mixed reality

Sitting between VR and AR is Mixed Reality (MR). It's like a blend of the best features from both worlds, creating a richer, more interactive experience.

Core Features:

- Hybrid Environment: MR merges real and virtual worlds to create new environments where physical and digital objects co-exist and interact in real-time.
- Advanced Interactivity: With MR, users can interact with virtual objects in the context of the real world. For example, a virtual ball can bounce off a real table.
- Spatial Awareness: MR devices are aware of their surroundings, recognizing objects and surfaces, and understanding the context of the environment.

Use Cases:

- Collaboration: Teams can collaborate in MR by interacting with 3D models or data visualizations in real space, enhancing productivity.
- Training & Education: MR can enhance hands-on learning. Imagine a medical student practicing a procedure with virtual guidance overlaid on a real-world training model.
- Entertainment: While still emerging, MR has potential in gaming and interactive

storytelling, blending our world with virtual narratives.

So, How Do They Differ?

- Reality Spectrum: Think of these technologies as points on a spectrum of reality. On one end, there's the real world. VR sits on the opposite end, representing fully digital realities. AR is closer to the real world, overlaying digital elements, while MR sits in the middle, blending both realities.
- Hardware: VR typically requires more substantial headsets, like the Quest 3. AR can often be experienced with just a smartphone, though AR glasses (including one from Meta). MR usually needs more sophisticated devices with spatial recognition capabilities; the forthcoming Apple Vision Pro is the best example–but that does VR too.
- Interactivity: While all three technologies offer interaction, the depth and type vary. VR is fully immersive with interaction inside a digital realm. AR offers basic

interaction between the real and virtual, and MR provides more advanced interactions between both worlds.

3 /
battle of the vrs

NOW THAT WE know what VR, AR and MR is, there's one more thing I want to dive into before talking about how to use the headset. I want to take a look at other headsets so you can get a better picture for how the Quest three is different.

meta quest 3 vs. meta quest 2

The most obvious place to start is putting Meta Quest 3 up against itself. How does it compare to the Quest 2 (the previous generation, which is still available at a cheaper price).

First and foremost, our eyes are in for a treat with the Quest 3. Sporting a resolution of 2,064 × 2,208 per eye, it's a noticeable jump from the Quest

2's 1,832 × 1,920. More pixels mean crisper visuals, allowing for a more immersive experience.

While both the Quest 2 and 3 support an experimental 120Hz, the baseline refresh rate of Quest 3 begins at 90Hz, which is a considerable improvement over Quest 2's starting 60Hz. Higher refresh rates can provide smoother visuals, particularly important in fast-paced games or applications.

The Quest 3 introduces pancake non-Fresnel optics, differing from Quest 2's single-element Fresnel. This change, combined with a slightly broader field-of-view, promises to offer a wider and more comfortable visual experience. Additionally, the Quest 3 offers a continuous IPD adjustment, catering to a broader range of users.

In the performance department, the Quest 3 gets a boost with the Snapdragon XR2 Gen 2 processor and a whopping 8GB RAM, compared to Quest 2's Snapdragon XR2 and 6GB RAM. More power and memory typically mean better performance and the potential for more complex VR experiences.

While both devices offer various storage options, the Quest 3 has an option for 512GB. If gaming and entertainment are important to you, you might want to opt into the beefier storage model.

Both headsets are quite similar in design, with the Quest 3 weighing just a tad more at 515g (compared to 503g for the Quest 2). While this isn't a massive difference, it's something to consider for those long VR sessions.

Battery life remains a crucial factor for untethered VR experiences. The Quest 3 offers a battery life ranging from 1.5-3 hours, which seems a bit less versatile than Quest 2's consistent 2-3 hours. If you are using this for productivity, the good news is you can use it while it's charging. If you are deadset on using it longer without charging, there are battery options.

Both headsets stick to the inside-out tracking mechanism, eliminating the need for external beacons. Notably, the Quest 3 boasts six external cameras, two more than its predecessor, potentially enhancing the tracking accuracy and overall experience.

The controllers have seen an update, with the Quest 3 featuring the Touch Plus compared to Quest 2's Touch v3. Hand-tracking and voice input remain standard on both. Audio-wise, both offer in-headstrap speakers and a 3.5mm aux output.

In terms of productivity, the passthrough feature is an important one–this lets you see the real world while you are using it. While both devices offer this, the Quest 3 steps up with a color pass-through compared to the Quest 2's low resolution black & white.

Finally, price. The Quest 3 starts at $500 for the 128GB variant, a bump from Quest 2's $300. However, considering the tech improvements and the inflation of tech commodities, the price increase seems justifiable for those wanting the latest and greatest.

meta quest 3 vs. meta quest pro

If your using this for work, you might be enticed by the sound of that "Pro" model. Becareful here, however. The Quest Pro may cost more, but it's also older technology. Let's look at how they compare.

Both headsets are powered by Qualcomm's Snapdragon XR2 series, with the Quest 3 featuring the XR2 Gen 2 and the Quest Pro boasting the XR2+. While both chips are designed for high-end VR experiences, the "+" in the Pro version hints at a slight performance edge.

The Quest 3 takes the cake with a resolution of 2064 × 2208, a noticeable bump from the Quest Pro's 1800×1920. Given that both utilize LCD screens, the Quest 3 promises crisper visuals, essential for immersion in VR.

The Quest 3's native 90Hz is coupled with an experimental 120Hz, promising ultra-smooth visuals. In comparison, the Quest Pro oscillates between 72Hz to 90Hz. Higher refresh rates can be kinder on the eyes, especially during extended use, giving the Quest 3 an edge in this department.

With a 110-degree field of view, the Quest 3 offers a slightly wider visual experience compared to the Pro's 106 degrees. A broader FOV can make a difference in immersion. As for the lenses, both headsets sport "Pancake" lenses, ensuring consistency in visual fidelity.

The Quest 3 comes packed with Touch Plus controllers, while the Quest Pro introduces the Meta Quest Touch Pro controllers.

At 515 grams, the Quest 3 is significantly lighter than the Quest Pro's 722g. If you've ever had a VR session that lasts hours, you'll know that every gram counts. The lighter frame of the Quest 3 might translate to more extended, comfortable play sessions.

While the Quest 3 boasts a respectable 8 GB of RAM, the Quest Pro steps it up with a whopping 12 GB. For heavy-duty VR applications and multitasking, that extra RAM could prove invaluable.

The Quest 3 offers two storage variants: 128 GB and 512 GB. On the other hand, the Quest Pro opts for a middle ground with a single 256 GB option. If you're a VR enthusiast with a vast library, the 512 GB Quest 3 might be calling your name.

meta quest 3 vs. pico 4

If you have budget on your mind, you've probably heard of the Pico 4 headset. It stacks up pretty well against the Quest 3. How much? Let's take a look.

The Meta Quest 3 and Pico 4 both feature variants of Qualcomm's Snapdragon XR2 processor. However, the Quest 3 has a slight edge with the XR2 Gen 2, which promises enhanced performance and efficiency. If horsepower is your top priority, Quest 3 is a whisker ahead.

Both devices offer 8GB of RAM, ensuring smooth multitasking and game performance. As for storage, the Quest 3 offers variants of 128GB and a whopping 512GB. Pico 4 doesn't lag far behind with its 128GB and 256GB versions. If you've got an extensive VR library, Quest 3's 512GB model is tempting.

Here's where things get interesting. While Quest 3 offers a resolution of 2064 x 2208 pixels per eye, the Pico 4 pushes slightly ahead with 2160 x 2160 pixels per eye. However, the Quest 3 boasts a refresh rate of 120Hz compared to Pico 4's 90Hz. In layman's terms, the Quest 3 promises smoother visuals, while the Pico 4 might deliver slightly crisper images.

With a 110-degree field of view, Quest 3 users will experience a marginally more expansive virtual landscape compared to the Pico 4's 105 degrees. Moreover, Quest 3's peak pixel density of 25 PPD bests Pico 4's 20.76 PPD, ensuring a more detailed visual experience.

Every gram counts in VR, especially during those binge-worthy sessions. The Quest 3, weighing 515 grams, is lighter than the Pico 4's 586 grams. A lighter headset usually translates to longer, more comfortable play.

Battery is where the Pico really is a decisive win for the Pico 4. With an estimated battery life of about 3 hours, it outlasts the Quest 3's 2.2 hours. For those who loathe frequent charging or plan extended VR sessions, the Pico 4 is a clear choice.

Both the Meta Quest 3 and the Pico 4 bring their strengths to the VR table. The Quest 3 excels with a smoother refresh rate, a slightly broader field of view, and potential performance enhancements. On the flip side, the Pico 4 shines with a marginally sharper display and longer battery life.

meta quest 3 vs. psvr 2

The focus of this book is productivity, but you can't talk about VR headsets without delving a little into gaming and entertainment. And because of that, it's worth taking a quick peak at PlayStations VR headset, the PSVR 2.

The Quest 3 boasts standalone functionality, meaning it doesn't need a PC to operate, although it does have PC link capabilities. In contrast, the PSVR 2 is closely tied to its parent – the mighty PS5. While the standalone feature of the Quest 3 offers portability and ease, the PSVR 2 leverages the powerful PS5 for top-notch VR experiences. The winner? Well, it's about preference: freedom vs. sheer power!

The Quest 3 sports an LCD display, while the PSVR 2 pulls out the OLED card. While LCDs usually offer brighter screens with power efficiency, OLEDs are known for their deeper blacks and vibrant colors. So, are you Team Crystal Clear or Team Vibrant Visuals?

The resolution race is tight here! The Quest 3 rocks a 2064 x 2208 resolution, slightly edging out the PSVR 2's 2000 x 2040. Although the difference might not be stark, every pixel counts when you're immersed in virtual worlds.

Both headsets are jamming at 120 Hz, ensuring buttery-smooth animations and reducing motion sickness. It's a tie in this department!

The Quest 3 starts at $499, undercutting the PSVR 2's $549. A $50 difference might not be deal-breaking for many, but for budget-conscious gamers, the Quest 3 takes the cake.

The Quest 3's full-color passthrough is a deal-breaker for those who wish to peek into the real world without taking off the headset. In contrast, the PSVR 2 doesn't come with this feature. Being able to see your surroundings, even in VR mode, gives Quest 3 a slight edge.

While the Quest 3 is powered by a next-gen Qualcomm Snapdragon, the PSVR 2 utilizes a beastly custom 7nm AMD Zen 2 CPU, shared with the PS5. If raw processing prowess is your jam, the PSVR 2 might be the way to go.

The Quest 3 starts off with 128GB. The PSVR 2, on the other hand, boasts a generous 826GB storage, although it's shared with the PS5. Still, in terms of sheer size, PSVR 2 takes the win.

In terms of productivity features, the PSVR 2 really can't compete; but what it does well–and even excels at–is in the game department. The games you'll find on PS5 have superior graphics.

meta quest 3 vs. apple vision pro

The real question on most people's minds is a headset that hasn't even come out yet: The Apple Vision Pro. Apple blew everyone's socks off when they showed off their spacial reality headset, which is due to launch in 2024. They also made everyone cry a little on the inside when they saw the cost! Lets take a look at both devices and see how they stack up.

Price is the real elephant in the room. The Meta Quest 3 comes in with a starting price of $499 for its base model, and $649 for its premium version. Apple Vision Pro, on the other hand, stuns with a whopping $3499 tag. This significant difference in pricing suggests that Apple may be targeting a different demographic, or banking on its brand appeal and potentially groundbreaking features.

Performance is crucial in VR. The Quest 3 sports the Snapdragon XR2 Gen 2, a powerful chipset designed specifically for VR applications. Apple, true to form, brings its proprietary hardware to the party with the M2 chip combined with an R1 chip. Apple's chips have consistently delivered top-tier performance in other devices, so expectations are high for the Vision Pro.

The Quest 3 offers variants of 128GB and 512GB

storage, paired with a solid 8GB of RAM. Apple's Vision Pro storage remains a mystery, labeled only as "TBD" (To Be Determined). The same goes for its RAM. It'll be intriguing to see where Apple lands in terms of storage, especially given the Vision Pro's premium price point.

Visuals in VR can make or break the experience. Both devices promise a treat for the eyes with 4K resolution displays. The Quest 3 boasts a "4K+ Infinite Display", with dual LCDs at 2,064 x 2,208 pixels per eye and a refresh rate of up to 120Hz. The Vision Pro keeps things simpler with a 4K resolution display for each eye, but specifics about its refresh rate are still under wraps.

The Quest 3 introduces a pancake lens optical stack, which should reduce the form factor while delivering sharp visuals. Apple, however, has partnered with Zeiss for its optical lens stack in the Vision Pro. Given Zeiss's reputation in the optics world, users might expect a visually impeccable VR experience.

Tracking accuracy is paramount in VR. The Quest 3 comes armed with six cameras, two MR sensors, and a depth projector. The Vision Pro, however, takes this a step further with a staggering 12 cameras, five additional sensors, and built-in eye tracking. The latter could hint at more intuitive user experiences and potentially adaptive visual optimizations based on where the user is looking.

The Quest 3 promises an approximate runtime of 2.2 hours, while the Vision Pro is a tad behind at around 2 hours. Given the high-powered hardware in both devices, it's understandable that battery life remains a challenge. Nevertheless, for extended VR sessions, every minute counts!

Should you save up for the Vision Pro? Time will really tell; early signs do point to it having a much clearer passthrough and more premium components–but how much that matters is going to depend on the user.

4 /
setup

mobile app setup

SETTING up the Meta Quest is a bit different than anything else you've ever did. You are probably excited to get it out of the box, but before you do that, download the Meta Quest mobile app from either the Apple App store or Google Play store. You'll need it during the setup.

After it's downloaded, you can either get started with unboxing the headset or create your Meta account. The order doesn't matter. You can only get so far before you have to add your device to the app, however.

device setup

Next, the moment you've been waiting for: using your headset. But first, you need to set that up. After you get all the paper removed, you'll want to press and hold the power button for three seconds (the power button is on the left side of the headset)--you'll here a chime when it's starting.

Next, remove the blockers that cover the battery on each controller. You can ture the controllers on by pressing either the button with the circle and three lines (

) or the button with what looks like a controller or Meta logo (

). There will be a blinking like and you'll get a vibration to indicate they're on. And if your wonder: yes, you can use your hands instead of the controllers, but you have to start with the controllers. I'll cover how to use your hands later in the book.

You can now put your headset on and begin the setup / tutorial. It's going to ask you to setup your wifi to, so you can start doing any necessary software updates.

Once you have your wi-fi in, one of the last steps will be adding your account by connecting it to the app.

On the app, you tap Menu in the bottom right corner, and then select devices.

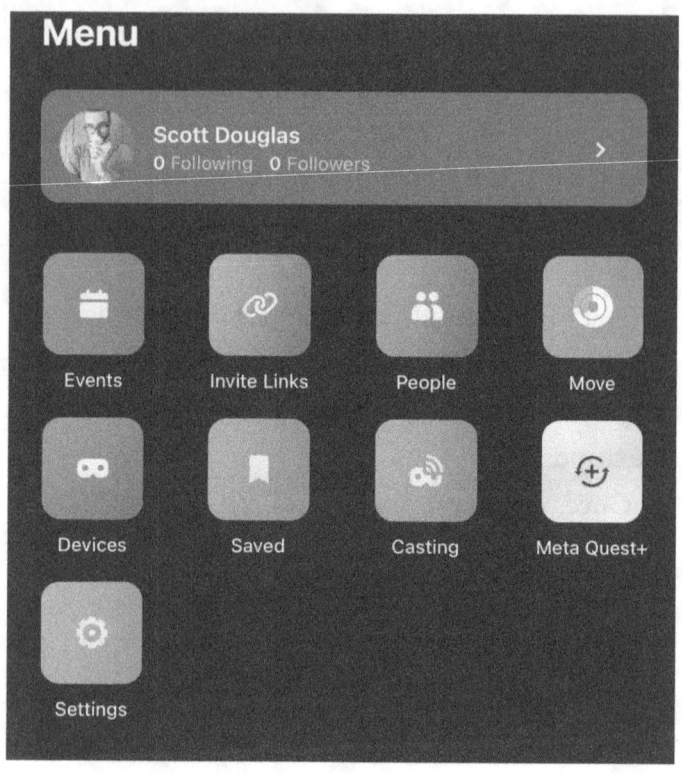

The app should automatically find your headset and controller (make sure bluetooth is turned on your phone and your on the same network). If all else fails you'll have to pair it manually. You can do this by putting the headset on and looking for the 5 digit pair code; take that code and add it into the app. Once you do that, the device should be paired and your set to go.

While your getting used to the headset, you might want to explore the Meta store from the app; anything you add from there will be added to the headset.

adjusting the straps

The Quest 3 is relatively like considering the power inside it. But wearing it several hours is going to give you strain. It's important to make sure you adjust the straps accordingly. Picking up additional accessories will also help–the comfort strap, for example.

You want to start by loosening the back strap by turning the knob. Get it secure over your head. From here, you can tighten the top strap by loosening the velcro and then pulling it back. Play with how it feels–adjusting the top strap correctly will take weight off other areas.

The two side straps can also be adjusted vertically and horizontally.

Finally use the knob in the front of the display to make visuals more clear.

It does take some getting used to, so it's best to wear it for a little, make adjustments and see if the adjustments help.

5 /
crash course

META QUEST 3 keeps things pretty simple in terms of the main menu; there's a lot here, so don't let the simplicity fool you; the idea of the menu is to help you get to where you want to go as quickly as possible. I'll talk more about navigation soon, but first, let's get familiar with the main areas.

You can access this main menu at any time by pressing the Quest button (

) on your right controller.

Below is the menu you should see on your headset.

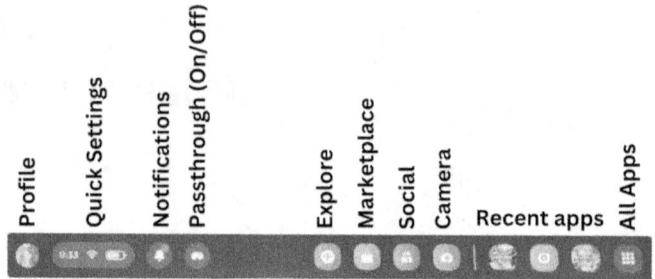

Now let's go over each of these areas.

Profile

Profile is where you go to see your—you quest it! Your profile. This is also where you would go if you have multiple people sharing the headset and want to switch accounts, or you want to change how your avatar looks (press Edit Avatar).

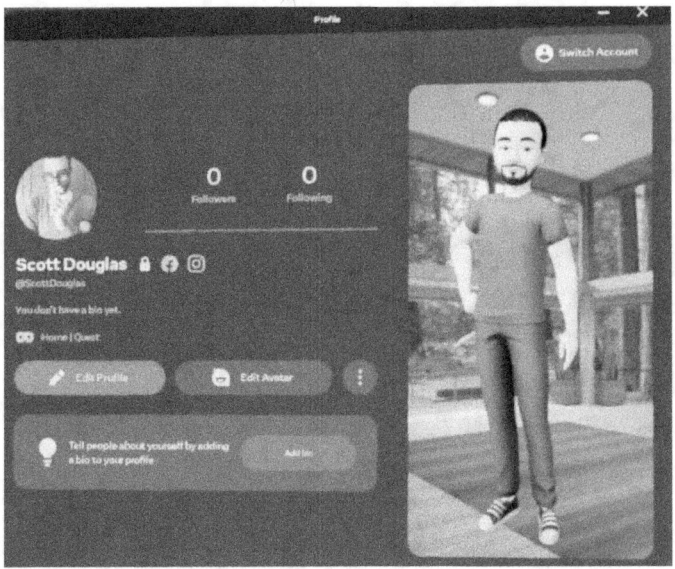

Quick Settings

Quick settings is where you can make quick customizations to your Meta Quest 3; if you need to change the wi-fi, for example, or the brightness of the headset. You can also go here to edit your boundary.

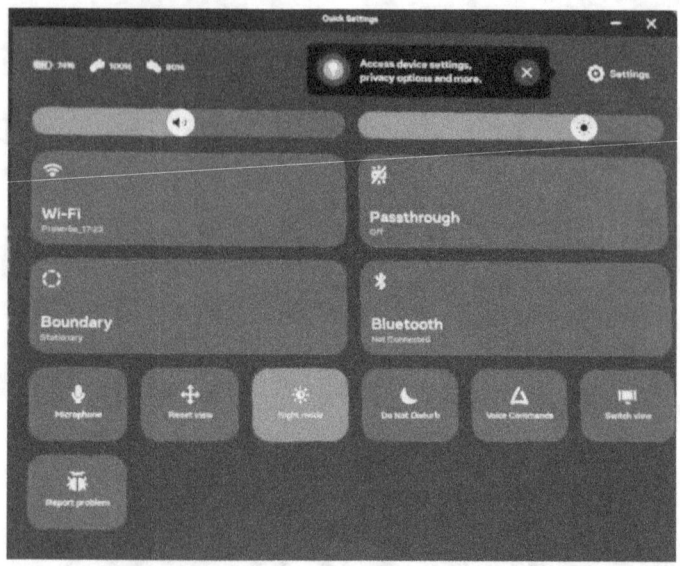

You can also go here to switch your view–there's two on the Quest: the normal flat view that you can easily move around, and the more curved one that is fixed on your screen.

Notifications

Go here to view notifications from apps, Messenger, and other apps.

Passthrough

The Quest has two main modes VR and MR. VR is when you are fully immersed–meaning you can't see your surroundings; MR is when passthrough is on: meaning you can see your surroundings. This toggles it on and off. You can also do this by tapping twice on the side of your Quest. This is a handy shortcut, so if you are playing a game you can quickly tap it to see if someone has entered the room.

Explore

Explore is not too different from the store / marketplace page; the biggest difference is Explore is more about recommendations.

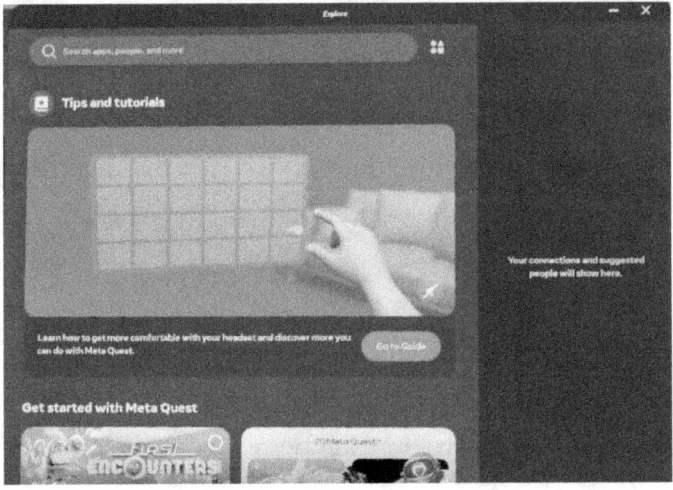

Marketplace

Marketplace, or store, is where you go to download apps; you can also do this on your phone. Anything you download on the Meta Quest mobile app will sync with your device.

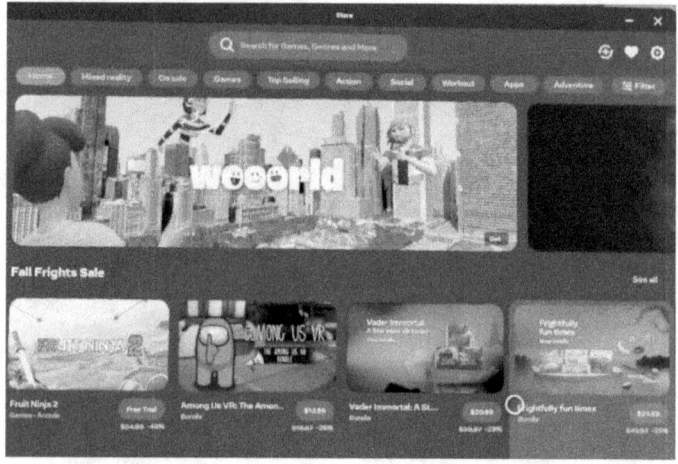

One of the most important things to know about the store: is the motion sickness rating. You've probably heard people say, "I don't want to do the whole VR thing because of motion sickness." It's a fair point, and the app store tries to help by giving a comfort rating. Green is comfortable; orange is moderate; and red means there is a definite risk for motion sickness if you are sensitive to that.

Social

The social (or People) app is where you can go

to hang out with friends–either to talk or to play games.

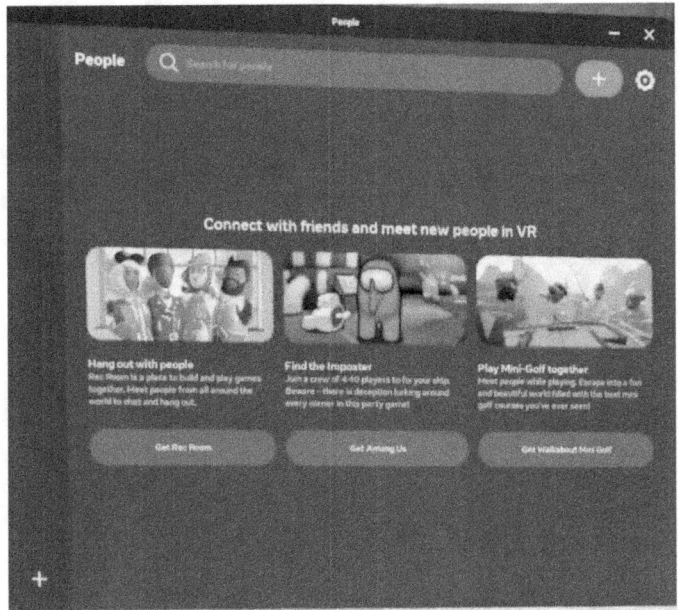

Camera

The camera shortcut lets you take videos and pictures with your device; just be aware they won't be the highest resolution.

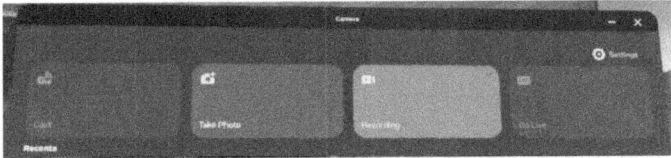

Recent Apps

Recent app is where the app you are currently using (or have recently used) will show up.

App Apps

All apps is the last option; this is where all of your apps show up.

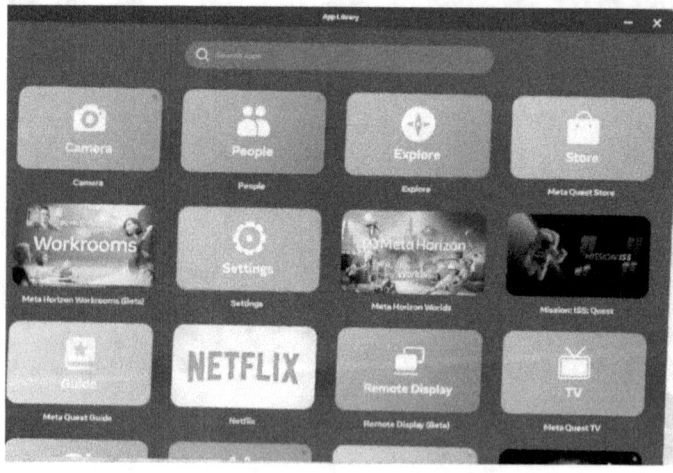

6 /
how to use

NOW THAT YOU know your way around the Quest 3, how do you actually use it? There are going to be three basic ways you move around: your controller, your hands, and your voice. Let's learn about each method.

controller navigation

Setup / Pairing

If you've never used the Quest, then you'll have to do a quick setup for the controllers. You've probably seen the little tabs sticking out of the controllers. Those are the battery blockers; batteries are already installed, so once you remove those, you should have a full charge (if you need to replace the battery, just push the button on the side and slide down. It takes a AA battery.

To turn on the controller, use the left controller and press the button with three lines

. The right controller is turned on by pressing the button that looks kind of like a controller (also known as the Meta button)

.

Within seconds, you should see an LED light, which means the controller is powered on. Put on your headset; go to Menu > Device and tap what you want to pair. It will walk you through it on screen (the first time you set up the device, it will be part of the initial onboarding; this is only for repairing). Once you pair them, you should see a blue light blink 3 times; that means it was successful. They'll automatically connect from hear on out.

Navigation

Now, how do you actually use the controller? It's going to vary depending on what app you are using, but generally speaking, this is what each button / mechanism represents.

The Thumbsticks is how you navigate around your environment.

The trigger button (this is the one on the front of the controller–not the one one on the side), or A and X button select objects in your environment.

B and Y will take you back to the previous screen / menu.

The controller button (or Meta button

) brings up the universal menu bar / dock. If you press and hold that button, it will recenter your headset.

The trigger-like button on the side of the controller is known as the Grip button; this grabs options or makes a fist with your virtual hands.

Finally, the button with the three lines (

) brings up the menu inside of apps.

direct touch navigation

Direct Touch navigation is when you use your hands instead of the controller; you can toggle between your hands and the controller by tapping your two controllers together or setting the controllers down.

Before you can do it, however, you have to first enable it by going into your Settings app and then selecting Movement Tracking. There are a few preferences there you can enable or disable.

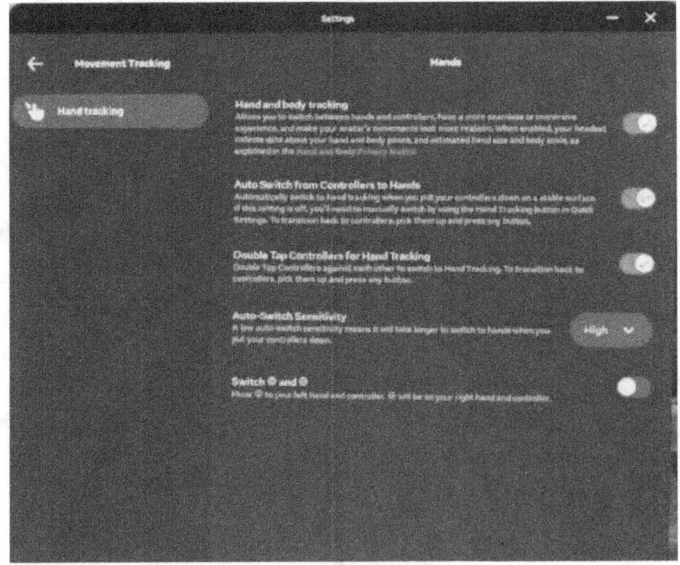

Using your hands isn't quite as intuitive as using controllers, and definitely takes some getting used to.

Use one finger to tap and select objects. You also use one finger to scroll and swipe if you are in a navigation menu.

You can move panels by going to their edge, waiting for them to highlight the borders, and then using your index finger and pinching with your thumb to move it or grab it.

To access the Quick Actions menu, look at the

palm of your hand and pinch your thumb and index finger together.

voice navigation

Voice Navigation is a little more intuitive since you are just using commands. Using it is pretty simple–press the Meta button twice (

) and then say your command.

Make sure it's enabled by going to Settings > System > Voice Commands.

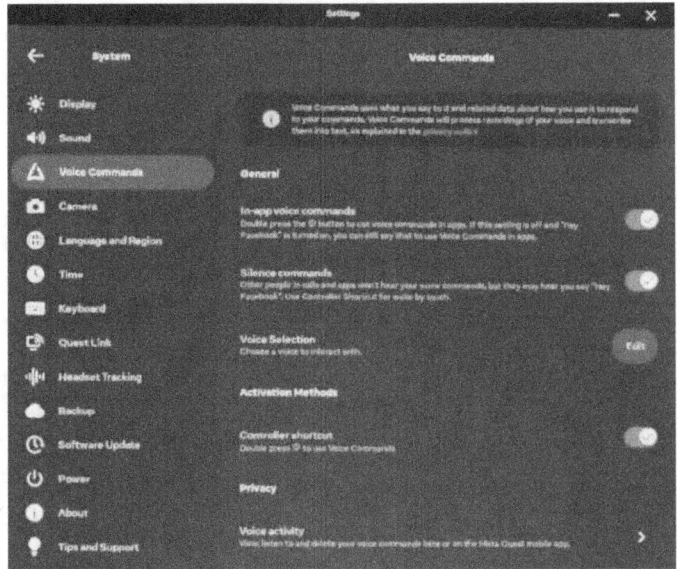

shortcuts you should know

Screenshots / Video Recording

To take a screenshot (albeit a not-so-great one, as you can tell by the ones in this book), hold the Meta button and pull the trigger once.

To take a video, hold the Meta button then pull and hold the trigger button until you see a message and a red dot that says the recording has started. Repeat to stop.

These screen and video captures will automatically sync with the mobile app when you are over Wi-Fi; go to the app, then gallery to view and download them.

. . .

Passthrough Mode

You can quickly toggle on passthrough mode (if you are immersed in a VR mode) by tapping twice on the side of your headset.

boundaries

Anytime you jump into a new space, the device is going to try and recommend boundaries based on what it sees; this helps make sure you don't hit or walk into things when you are immersed in a VR environment. You can edit the boundary before accepting it. You can also draw your own boundary or use a stationary boundary (ideal if you are sitting).

web browsing

The Quest 3 can be used for casual web browsing. It's all done in the Meta Quest Browser, which is already installed on your headset.

The browser probably will look familiar. It's based on Chrome. It's very simple to use. Press inside the address bar, and an onboard keyboard pops open. Use the plus to open a tab, the banner to bookmark, and the three dots on the far right to open more options.

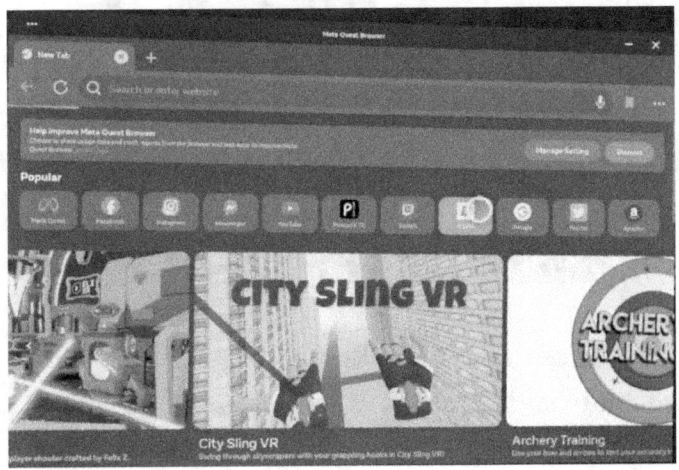

Bookmarking a page will bring up the following window; once you press save, it will go into your Bookmark folder.

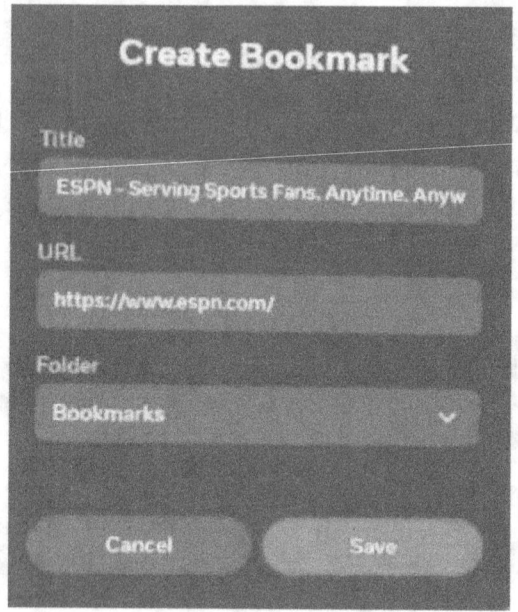

You can access the Bookmarks at anytime, but clicking on the three dots to bring up the expanded menu.

There's not a lot in that expanded menus area. You can see downloads, history, change settings, and clear data.

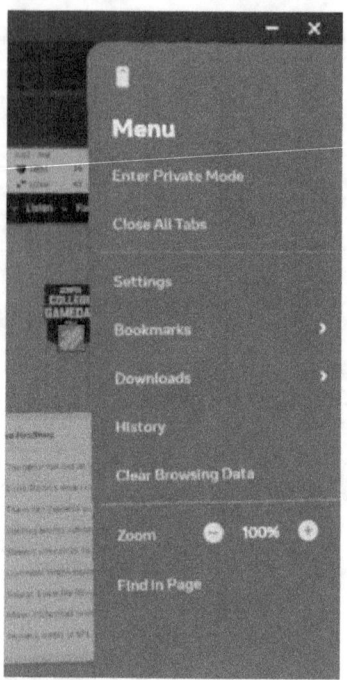

The one you might want to use is private mode. When you're in private mode, it hides your history. I typically use it when I'm shopping for gifts and don't want people in my house to know what I've shopped for. To exit private mode, just click on the X. Normal mode should come back up.

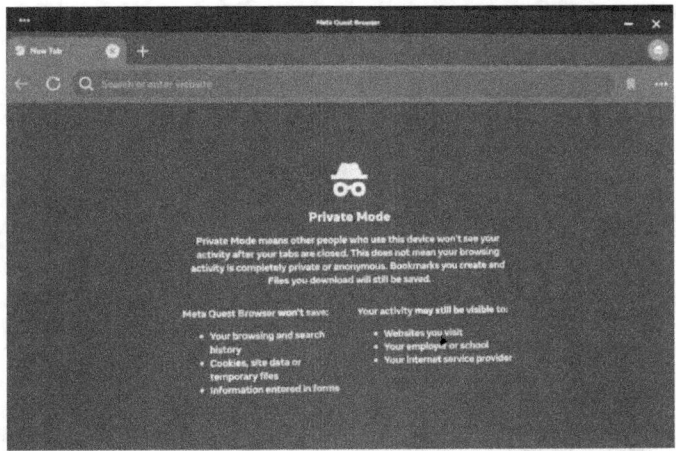

youtube vr

In terms of media players, the one I recommend is YouTube VR. It's free and has an interface that you've probably seen and used hundreds of times.

When you open it, you'll see all kinds of 360 videos–360 means you get a fully immersed experience where the movie is literally all around you (and above and below you). When you play a normal video, you'll have a couple of options in that config button on the right side. The two of note: are curved screen (your screen can either be curved or straight–try both and see what your preference is) and screen size (there are three to pick from). If you are in a small space, you probably won't like the largest one.

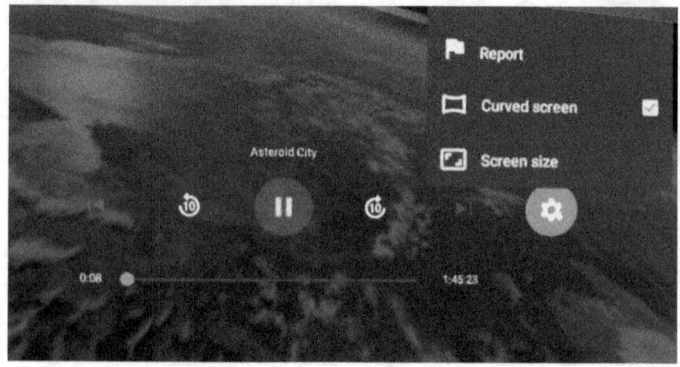

One reason I'm a huge fan of YouTube VR: Movie Anywhere. Did you ever get one of those Blu-rays (or perhaps you still do), and they include a redemption code for Movie Anywhere? You can sync that with YouTube through Google Play. That means your entire catalog of movies can play on the Quest 3! If you've bought digital movies on iTunes, Amazon, or other retailers, then sync Movie Anywhere there as well–sometimes, when you buy a digital copy, it will sync up there. You'd be surprised how many movies are compatible.

working in vr

WHEN IT COMES to working remotely on Quest 3, you have a few different options, but only one is built into the Quest 3: Virtual Desktop.

remote display

When it comes to working remotely, your first option is Remote Display. Remote Display comes preinstalled on your Quest 3.

You'll find it when you open up All Apps.

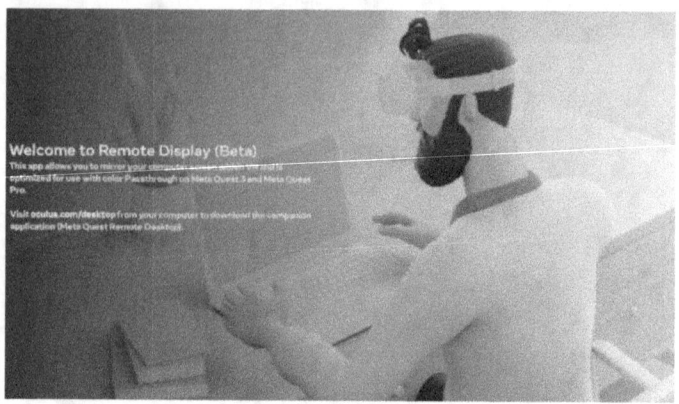

Before you can use it, however, you'll need to download Meta Quest Remote Desktop on your Mac or PC. Once you have it installed, turn on your Quest 3 and put it near your Mac or PC; it should find it quickly if it's turned on.

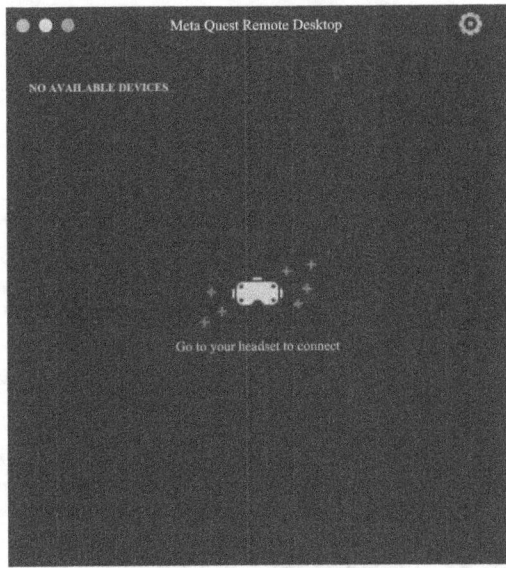

You only have to add your computer once; once it's paired it will look for it whenever the appis open.

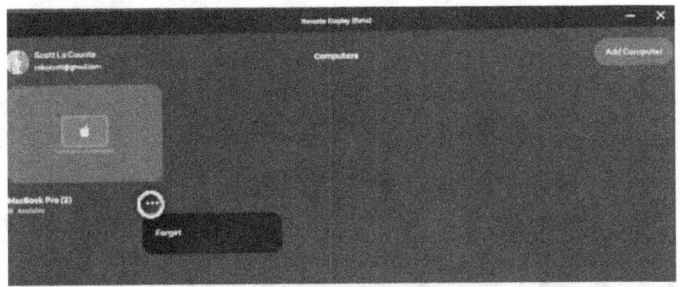

Remote Desktop is pretty limited. If you really want to take advantage of working in the VR space, then download Workrooms, which is free and developed by Meta.

workrooms

Workrooms is a much more immersive space, and lets you add screens and really take advantage of the space around you.

To get started, you have to download Workrooms to both your Quest 3 (by getting it from the app store) and your Mac or PC.

First thing you'll see is a message about clearing

your space. It sounds silly, but it's important. Once you start using the space, you'll kind of forget your in it and it will be easy to knock things over.

Once your computer is installed, you'll have to configure the space. A tutorial will walk you through it, but essentially, you are using your controller to highlight over the area of your desktop space.

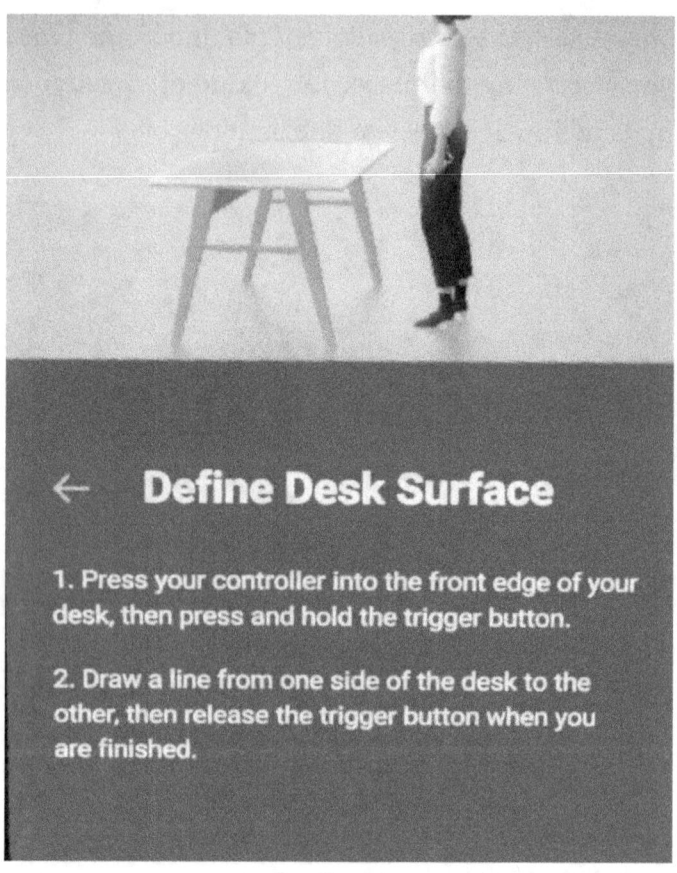

Once the area is defined, you'll point your controller down and push down to the the correct height.

Once setup, you'll see your computer screen in front of you, a little menu box below it, and a virtual keyboard that looks like your computer. You can use your physical keyboard and mouse in this space; this is just a visual representation of it, but does not actually work.

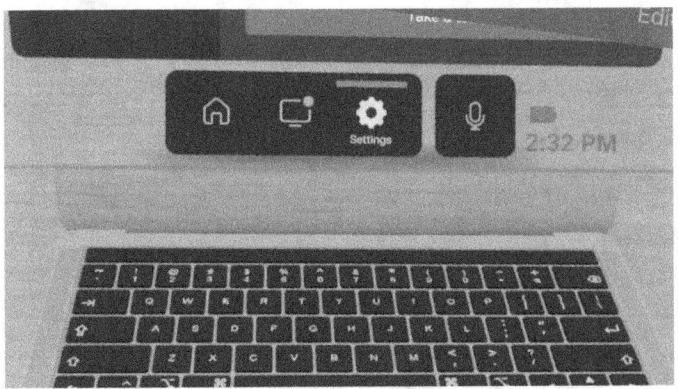

The menu has three options:

Office - where you can your schedule (Today),

your computers (Rooms) and change the environment (Customize Office).

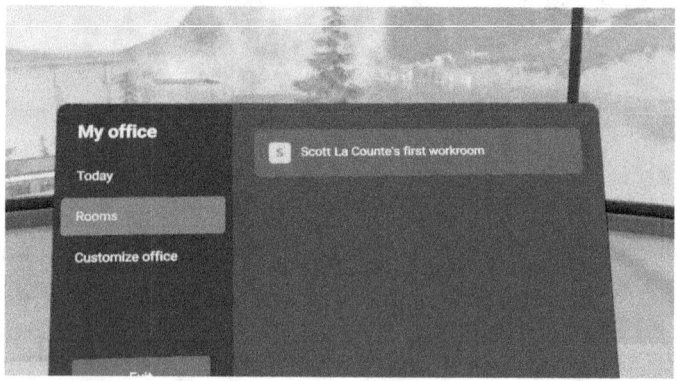

Computer - This is where you can add additional virtual screens. What's a virtual screen? It extends your computer's screen so it can have up to three.

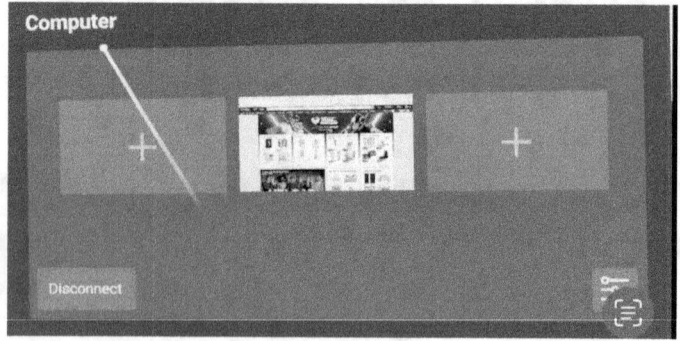

Once you press a + on either side, you'll see the screens added immediately. You can also touch and grab a screen and move it. So if you want the center screen on the left or right, for example.

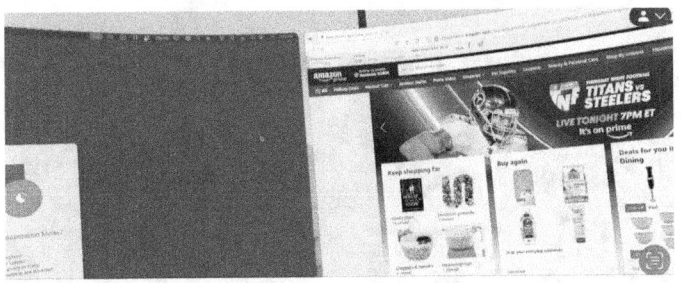

If you press the customize in the lower right corner, there's a few settings in here that you can update. If you don't want your computer to connect automatically (which is the default), then just press the toggle.

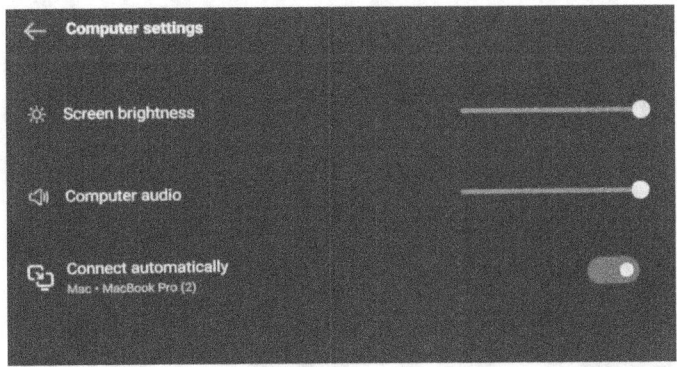

Settings - Finally, settings lets you change your Avatar (if you want a different look), Desk (if you need to reconfigure it), and profile, which lets you update your username that others who come into your workspace would see.

You might completely miss it at first, but there's two more menu options; you have to look down to see them. They're in the bottom right corner. The top button is passthrough (if you want to use your workroom in passthrough mode) and the other is Desk Whiteboard.

When you are using the Desk Whiteboard, you

can turn your controller downward and scribble on the black pad. You can use this to jot notes, create sticky notes, and more.

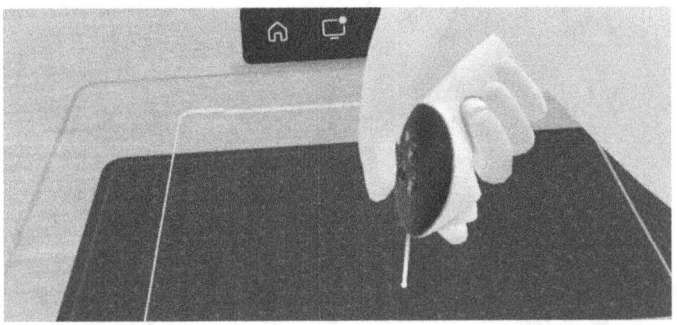

other options

I'm doing my best to focus on apps created by Meta in this book, but when it comes to virtual computing, you have more options. The most popular is Immersed (immersed.com); while there is a free plan, to take full advantage of it, then you'd want to switch to the paid one–$10 a month. Paying lets you add more than 3 displays.

8 /
settings app

NEXT, let's dig into how you make changes to the settings of your headset. You won't go in here often, but you probably will spend some time here when you first get the device; for the most part, it's a one-and-done app, but it's helpful to know where things are.

You can see in the image below that there are a *lot* of options. Most will be in the System section, however.

system

What's in the Systems menu? Let's find out?

display

If you've watched a few videos on the Quest 3, you might heard someone talk up 120 Hz refresh rate. Awesome, right! If your a novice to this thing, you might be scratching your head. What is 120 Hz refresh rate, and do you need it?

Refresh Rate refers to the rate refers to how many times a new image can appear; the faster the refresh rate, the faster it appears; this is important on things like scrolling and transition–or in motion if you are playing games. You obviously want a fast refresh rate, right? Yes and no, which is why you see a toggle switch in the Display. 120 will make everything look all snappy...except your battery supply–because a fast refresh rate means a faster battery drain.

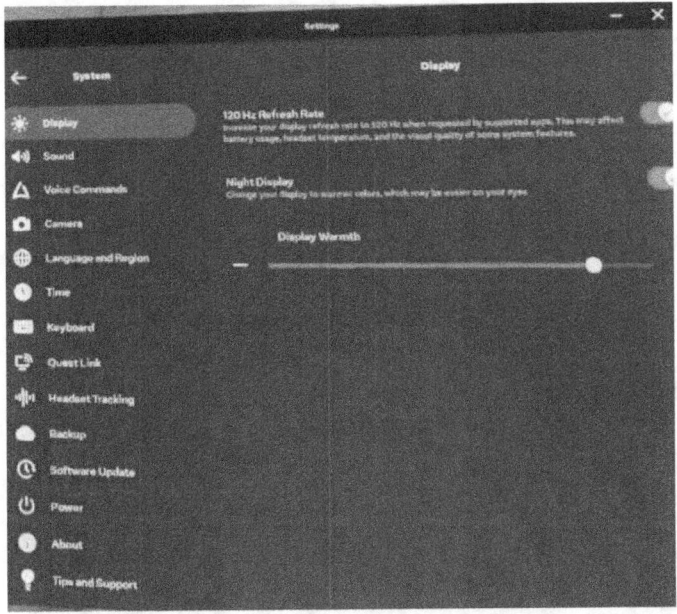

You can also turn on and off Night Display; personally, I leave it on. It makes everything darker, which for me is easier on the eyes. Under that is the warmth, which also can help when you are using the headset for extended time.

sound

Sound is pretty basic–you can turn on and off the sounds you'll hear if you get a message, or mute your microphone. You can also turn on Do Not Disturb, which will mute all incoming sound.

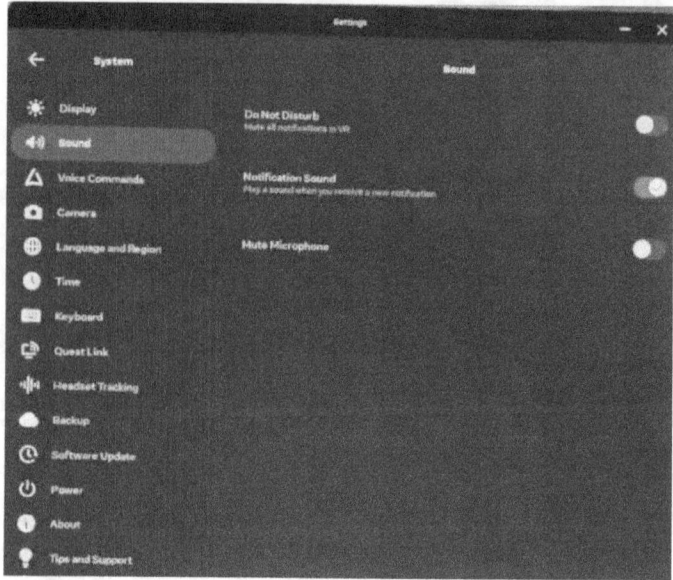

voice commands

Earlier, I mentioned controlling the headset with your voice; this is where you turn that on and off.

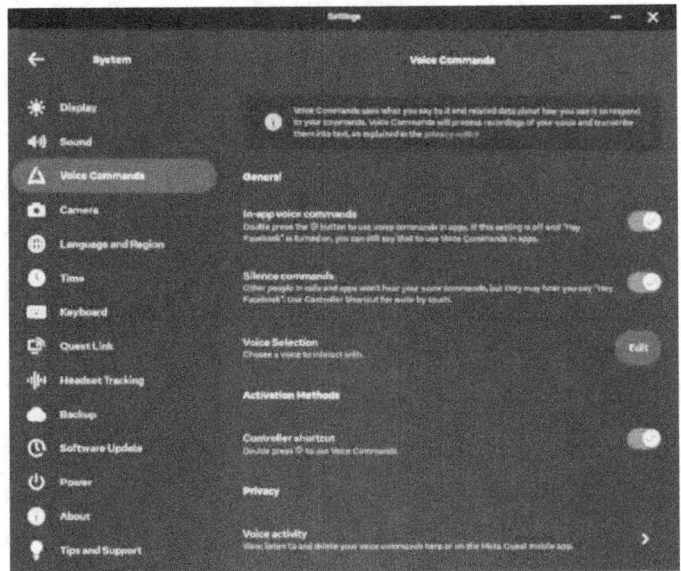

You can't do everything with your voice, but you can do a lot. Here are some examples:

Device

- "Shut down the Quest."
- "Restart the Quest."
- "Turn up the volume."
- "Lower the volume to [specific number]."
- "Reset view."
- "Go home."
- "Reset Guardian."
- "Change to roomscale."

- "What's my battery?"
- "Enable Hand Tracking."
- "Take a screenshot"
- "Record a video"

Apps

- "Find some racing games."
- "Show adventure games."
- "Find action games."
- "Open [some website]."
- "Open Library."
- "Open [specific game]."
- "Close game / app."

Playing Media

- "Show me 360 videos."
- "Find cat videos."
- "Next."
- "Previous."
- "Play."
- "Pause."
- "Start casting."
- "Stop casting."
- "Open camera roll."

- "Take a photo."
- "Start recording."
- "Stop recording."

Social

- "Open messages."
- "Send a message."
- "Who's online?"
- "Start a party."
- "Open parties."
- "Show me events."

Help

- "What can I say?
- "How do I change my profile picture?"

Fun

- "Tell me a joke"

Weather

- "What's the weather next week?"
- "Is it raining?"

- "When is sunset?"
- "Is it hot?"

Info

- "Convert ten miles to kilometers."
- "Convert ten degree Celsius to Fahrenheit."
- "What day is it?"
- "What is 4 times 4?"
- "Who won the Oscar for best picture in 1981"
- "When was George Clooney born"

camera

The Quest 3 doesn't exactly have stunning photo resolution, but it does have the ability to take photos and videos. You can change how it captures them and the quality in this section of settings.

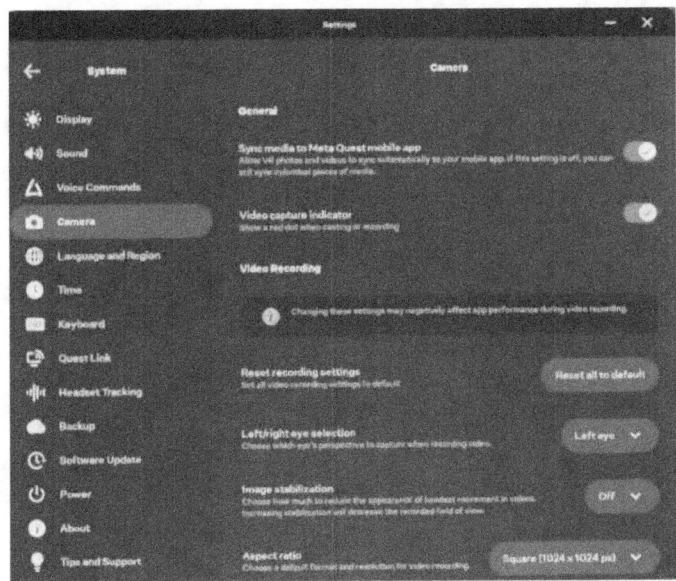

language and region

If you need to change the language or the metric for how temperature is recorded, you can do so here.

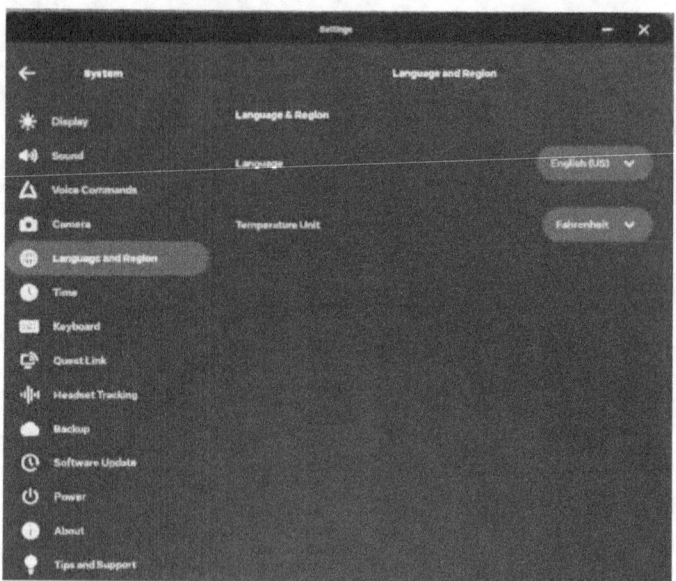

time

By default, time is set automatically based on your location; if you'd like to do it manually for whatever reason, then you would go here.

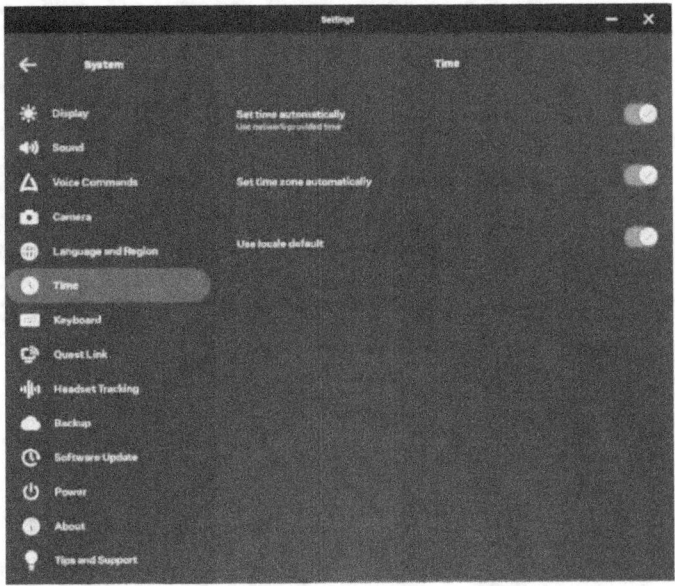

keyboard

There aren't a lot of options in the keyboard, but it does let you enable or disable it you are contributing to improvements. This section is only in reference to the headsets onboard keyboard–not any keyboard you assign via Bluetooth.

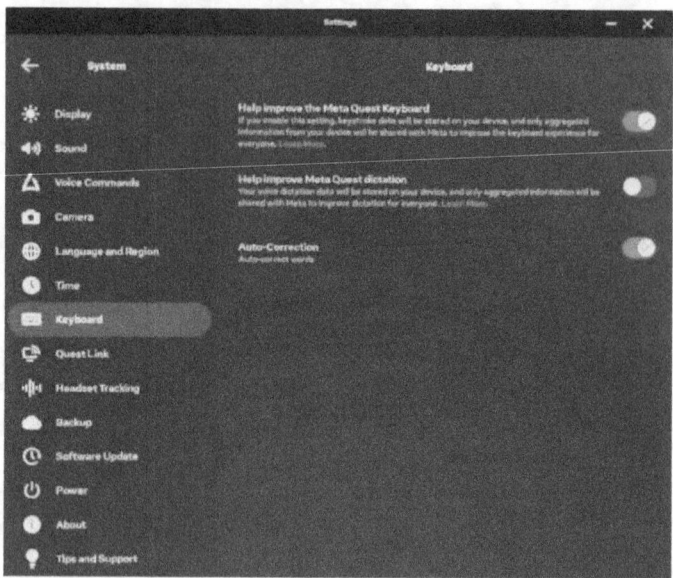

quest link

If you are a PC gamer, than Quest Link might be for use. If you purchase the Quest Link cable and plug it into your PC (sorry Mac and Linux users, this one isn't for you) you can turn your headset into a PCVR headset. It essentially uses your PCs power.

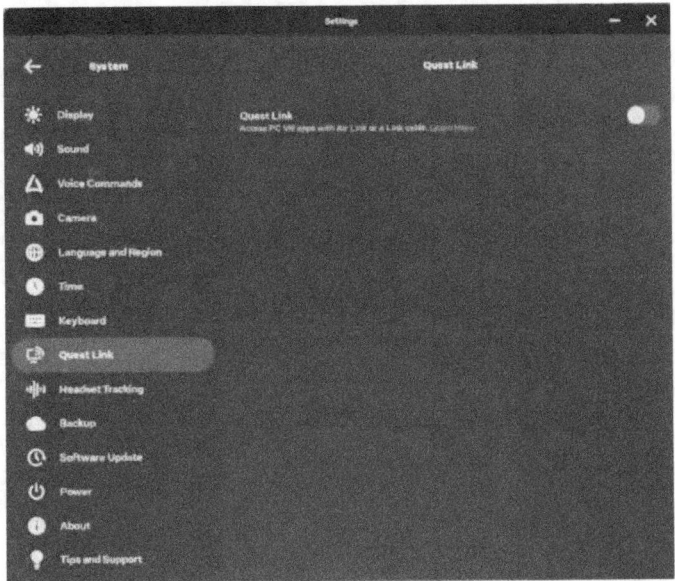

headset tracking

This section enables how your headset is tracked. It's tracked by default and that's probably where you want to keep it.

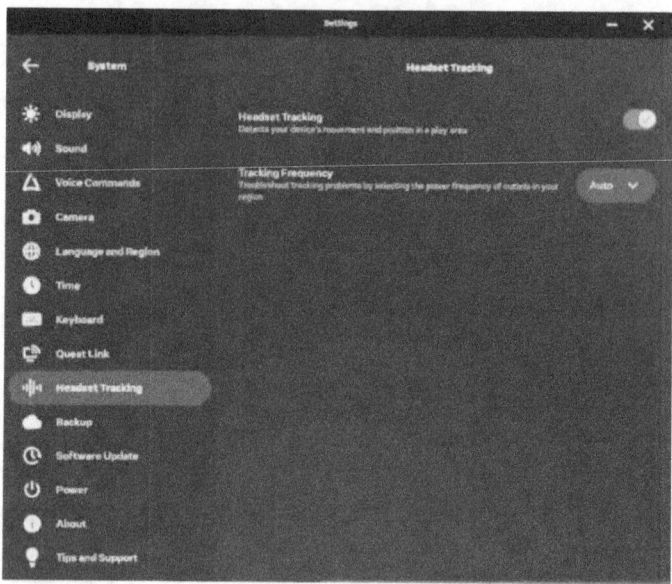

backup

This is a simple toggle (enabled by default) that has your headset back everything up over the cloud. It's a good idea to just keep it on unless you have an edge case for why you might want it off.

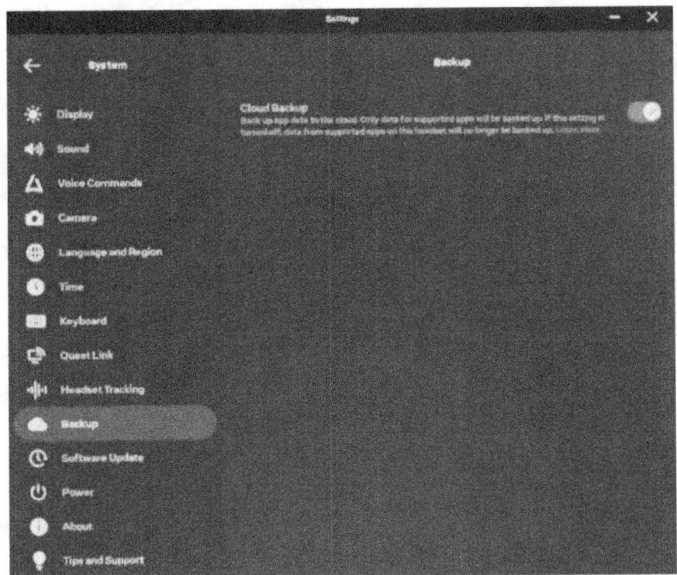

software update

A few times a year, Meta will release updates to the headset; this is where you view them; it's a good idea to do them when they become available. Sometimes they are security updates meant to protect you against vulnerabilities.

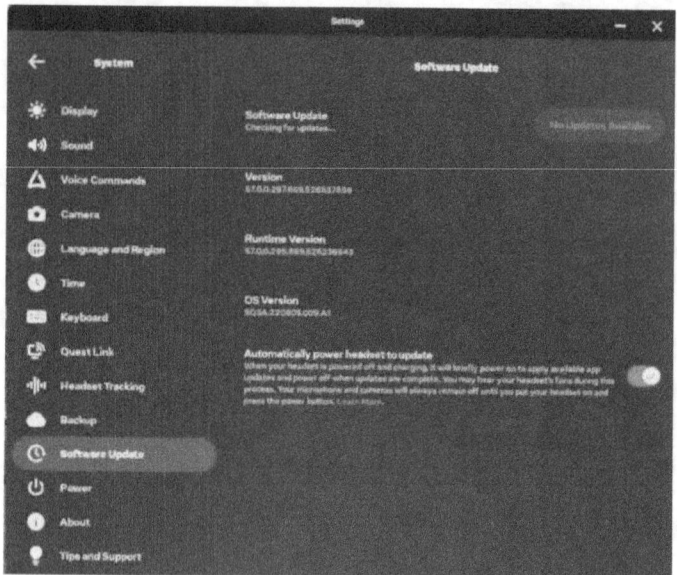

power

If you want to get the most out of your headsets, then this is a section you'll want to navigate to. There are only two options here, but both are meant to extend your battery life. The first is just when your device goes to sleep if not being used; the second will make tweaks to optimize your headset's performance–which means it might not run as well (it's kind of like Low Battery mode on an iPhone).

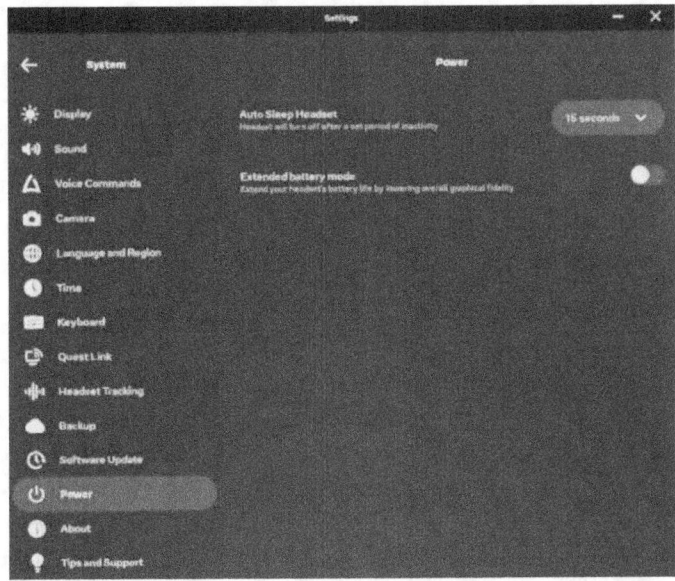

about

There's nothing most users will need in the About section; it gives a few technical details (like the mac address) and links to terms of service and privacy policy.

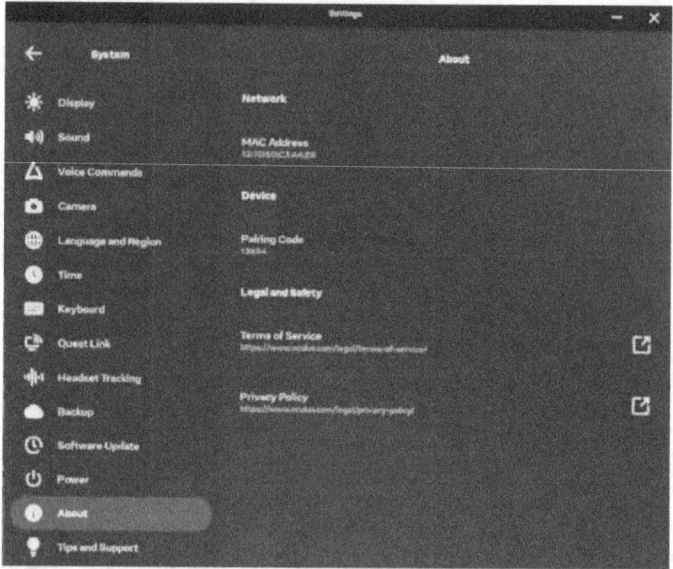

tips and support

There's nothing to do in Tips and Support–and it might surprise you to know that there actually aren't any tips in this section. There are two things that you can do here, and both take you to external sites. The first is to report a problem, and the second is to get support.

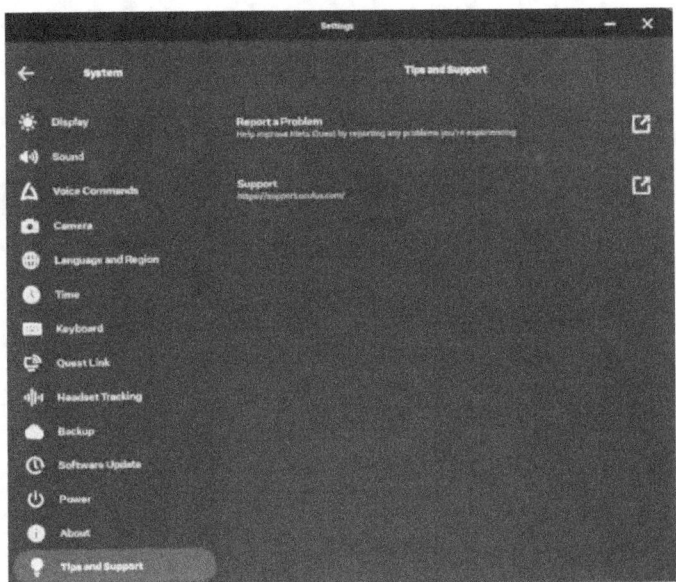

physical space

Physical space is about the settings that pertain to what's around you; it's not to create a boundary, but rather it's to make adjustments to the boundary that is or will be created.

Boundary

Your Boundary is the space around you; it helps make sure you don't hit things. This isn't to create your boundary. It will let you set the ring color and adjust the boundary sensitivity, however.

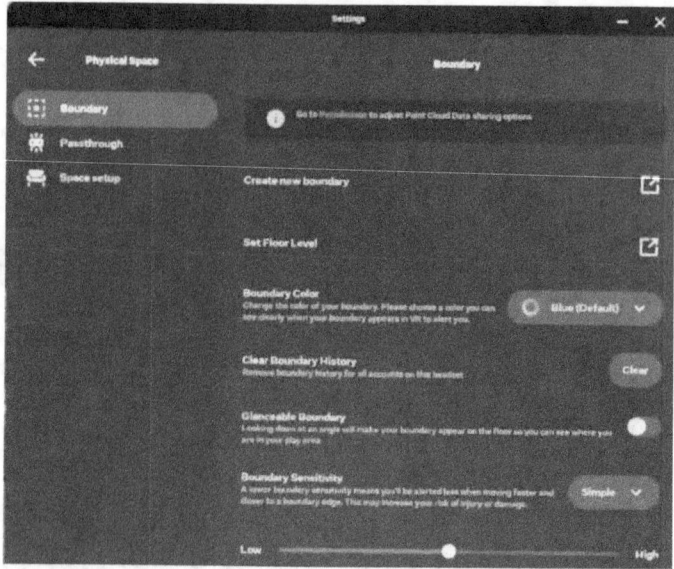

Passtrough

The easiest way to turn on Passthrough mode is by tapping your headset twice. Don't like that? You can turn it off here.

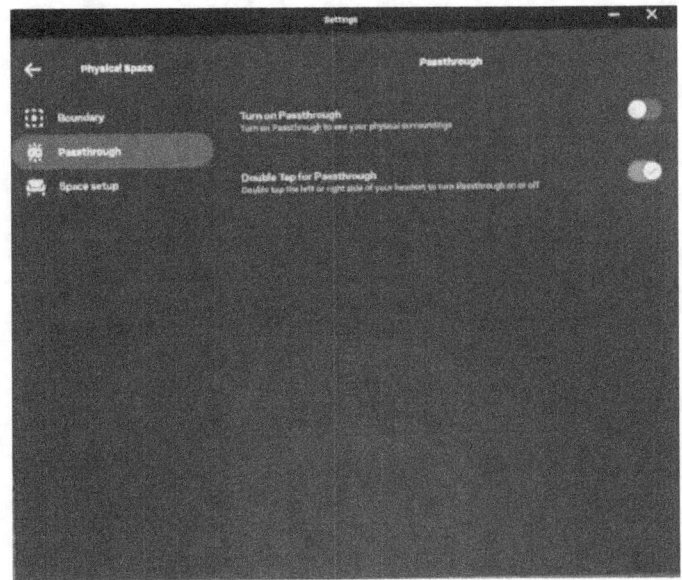

Space Setup

Boundaries is helpful for VR; Space Setup is more for MR. Unlike boundaries, you can setup your Space here–press the setup button.

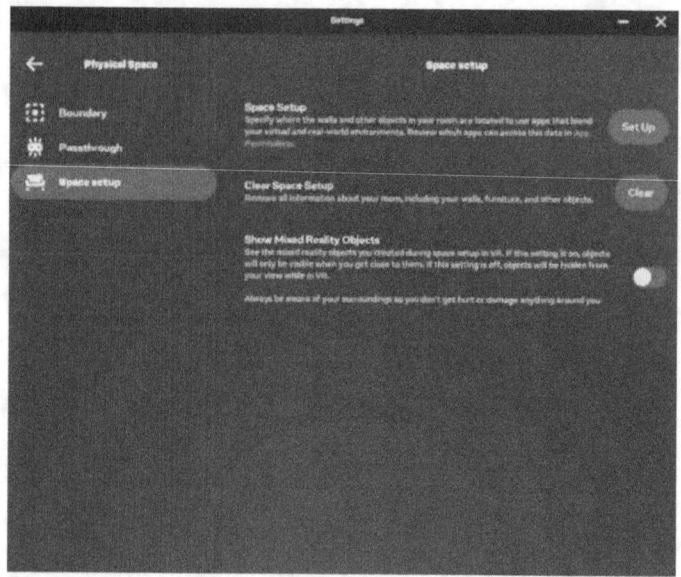

wi-fi

What if you decide to take your headset out of the house and need to put it on a different wifi? You can make a change to your wifi here.

personalization

How your environment looks is basically like your desktop wallpaper–but it's 360. There's a lot you can do to make your space feel more like you– including downloading environments on the web.

Virtual Environment

The most obvious change is the visual environment–or your background. There's a lot of choices here, but you can also get them on the Internet.

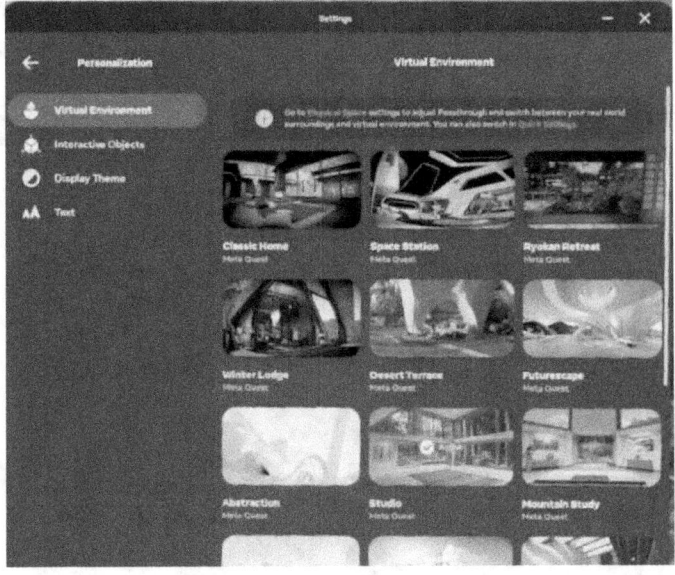

Interactive Objects

There's not a lot in this section–just two toggles you can turn on and off.

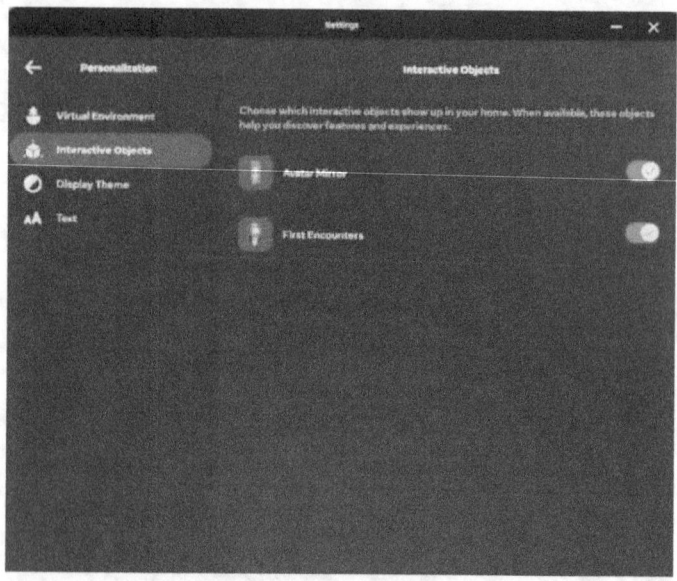

Display Theme

Your display theme is all the colors you'll see on the device–think about button colors, menu bar colors, and text colors. You can change most of that.

Text

Finally, Text is where you'll go to change the size of the text. If you want things bigger or smaller, then you'll change it here. It's one of the first sections I went to because it helped make things more readable on the device.

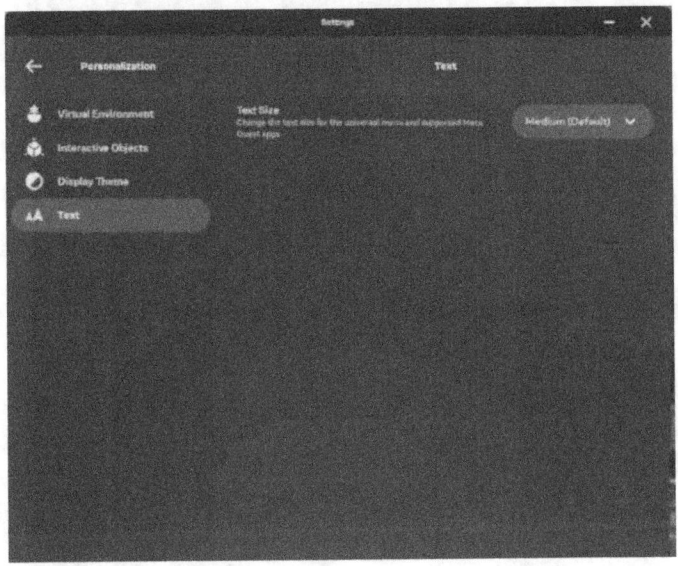

storage

When you first get your Meta Quest 3, storage won't seem like a big deal. You got plenty of it! Give it a few days, and then you might change your tune. Once you start installing things, it adds up pretty quickly.

This section lets you quickly visualize where all your storage is going, and remove games and other applications that you don't use and are taking up a lot of space.

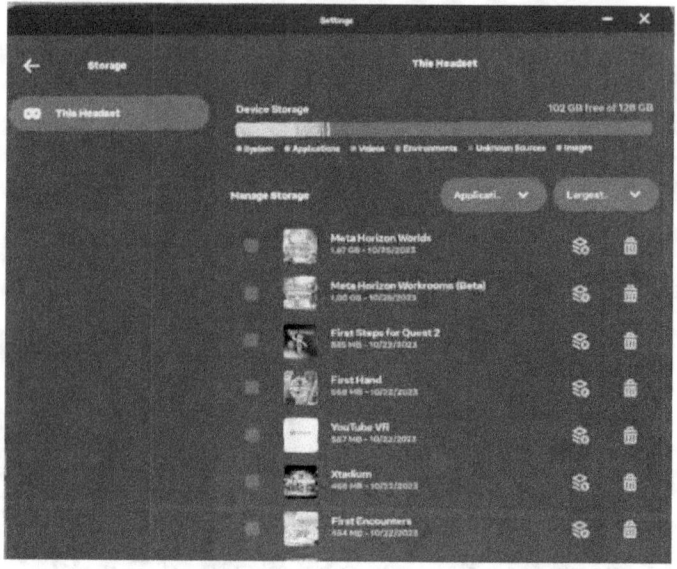

apps

The Apps section is more about what your applications can and can't see and who can access them, then what the applications actually are.

Permissions

Permissions is the first section, and this lets you modify what apps can and can't see. If you don't want them to be able to use your camera, for example. Sometimes these permissions are required to use the apps, and sometimes, developers just add them in because they're lazy.

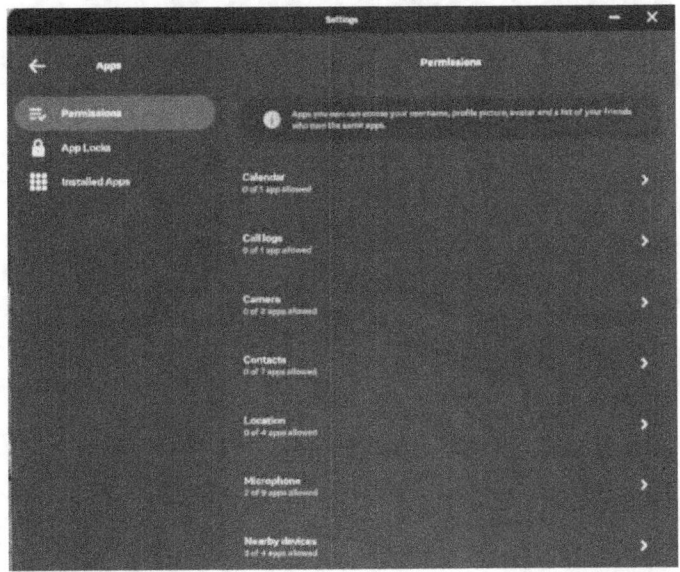

App Locks

Somethings on your device might be for your eyes only; maybe it's a game with violent content, or just a virutal computer you don't want others to see. You can use this section to lock them so you need a pattern to open them.

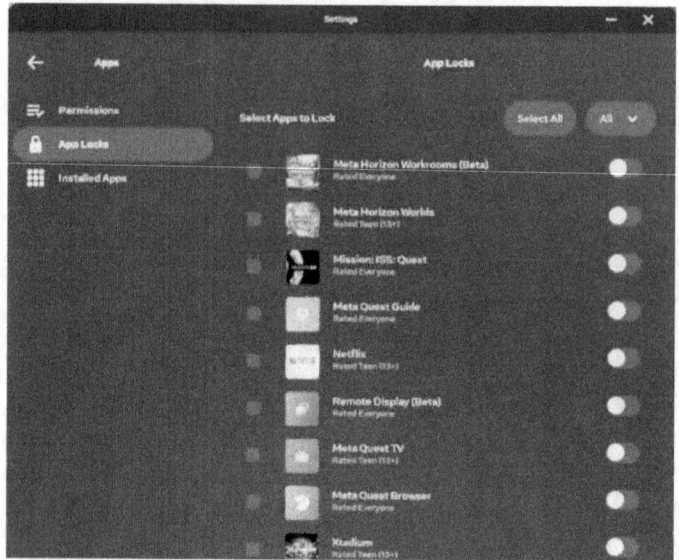

Installed Apps

Finally, installed apps lets you see what's on your device and make changes to them.

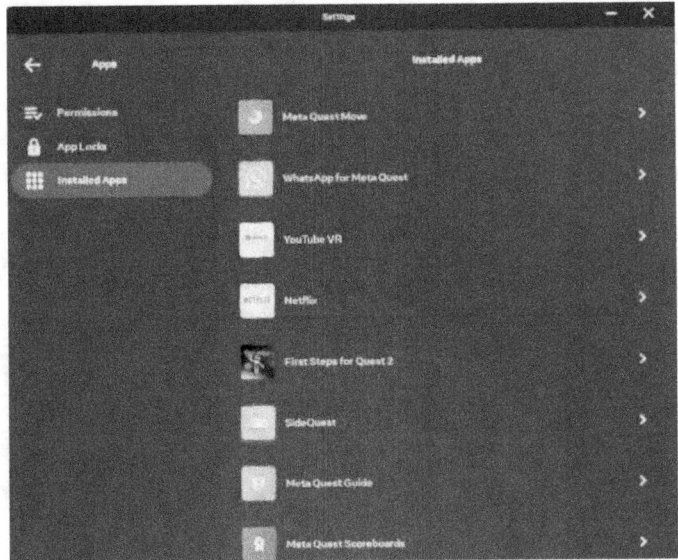

notifications

Notifications lets you update what apps can send you notifications; the toggle you'll use most, however, is do not disturb. Use that toggle anytime you want to silence all notifications.

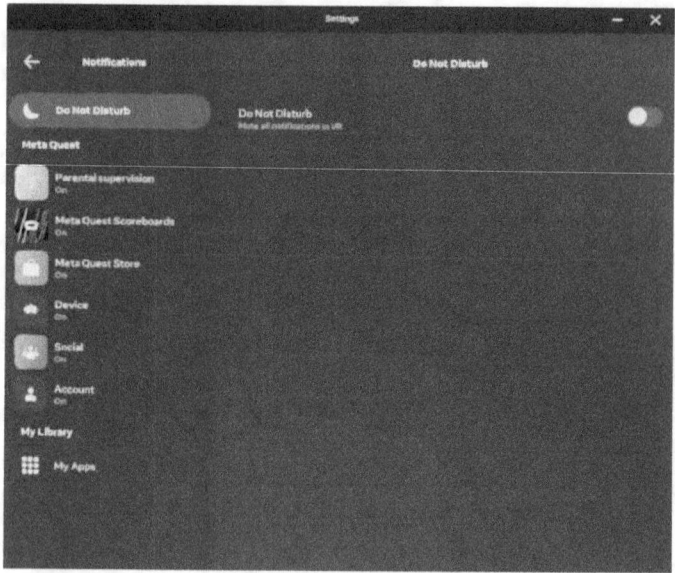

accounts

One of the nice things about the Quest 3 is you can share it with other people; you can add up to three users on the headset. Just click the Add Account button. You can also share purchased content with them by toggling it on. Just be mindful that you'll go through storage quicker with multiple users.

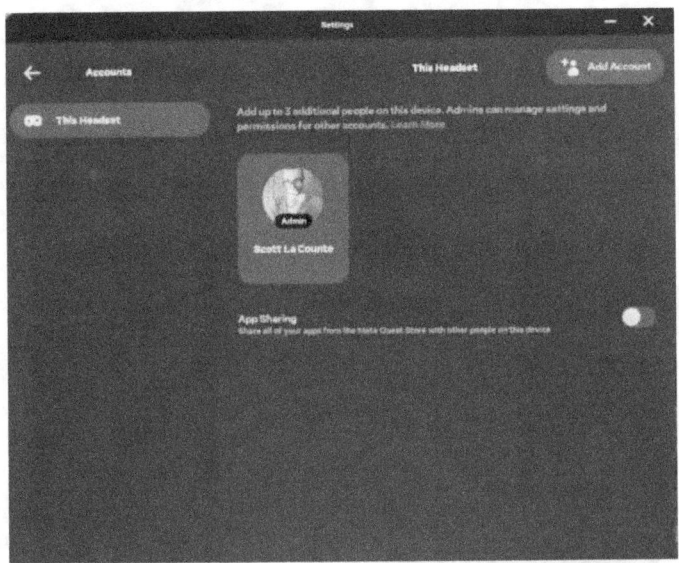

To switch users, press the Meta button to pull up the menu bar, and then click the profile avatar on the far left side. In the box that opens, select Switch Profiles in the upper right corner.

devices

If your planning on using your headset to do productivity, then this section is a big one. This is where you can pair and adjust how you use all the devices like a keyboard and mouse to your headset.

Bluetooth

Before you can make adjustments to your

devices, you need to add them. Select the Pair button when you are ready. Most bluetooth devices have some kind of button that you'll press and hold to get started.

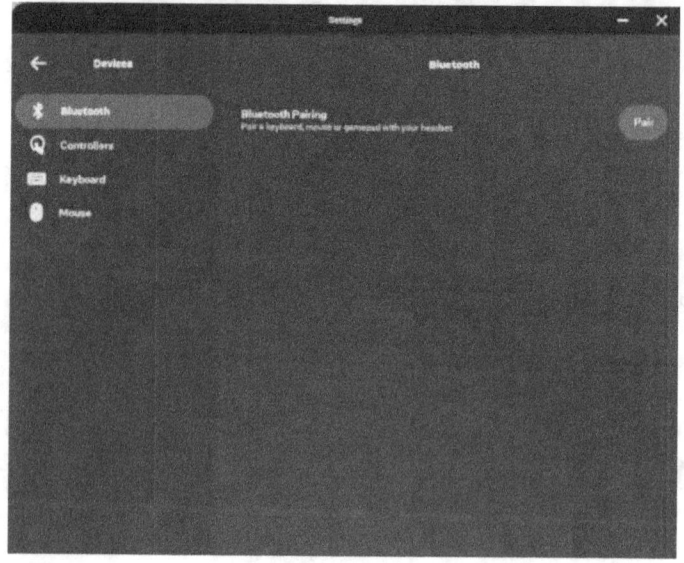

Controllers

Once you have something connected, you can start adjusting how it's actually used on your headset. Controllers, for example let's you change buttons on a controller you have connected to the Quest. And yes, you can connect Xbox and PS5 controllers.

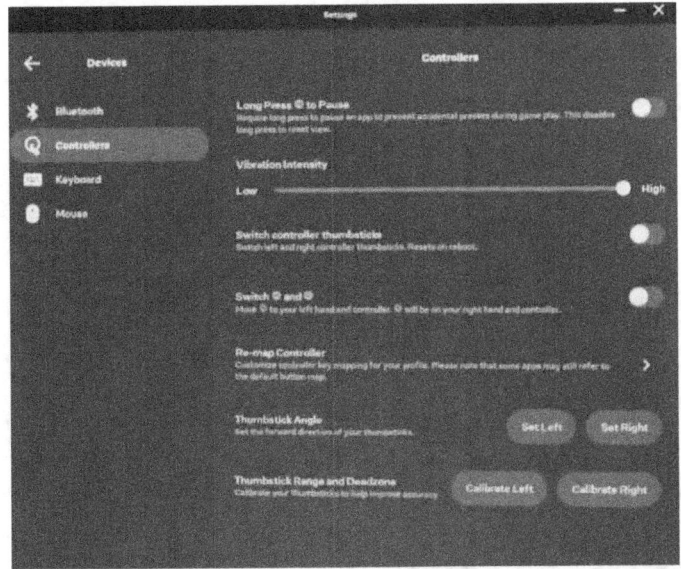

Keyboard

Keyboard lets you make changes to both a physical (Bluetooth) keyboard and a VR keyboard.

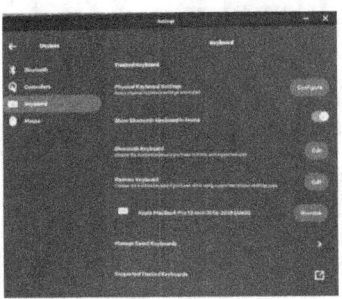

Mouse

And finally mouse let's you change things like

how responsive a mouse is and how large the
cursor is.

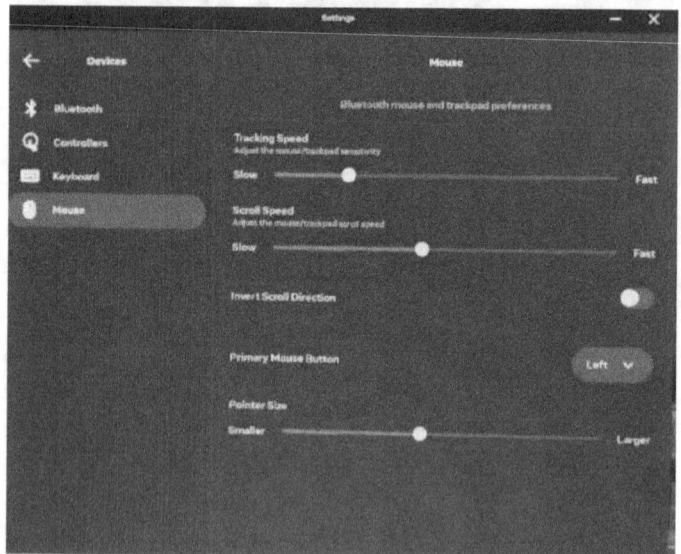

movement tracking

You probably have seen some videos about the
Quest 3 letting you use your hands; you probably
saw more people talk about it after the Vision Pro
was shown off (the Vision Pro has no controllers);
by default, it's not turned on. Controllers is the
most accurate way to control your Quest, but you'll
probably want to switch to your hands at some
point; Movement Tracking is where you toggle it
on and tell the Quest how you want to activate it.

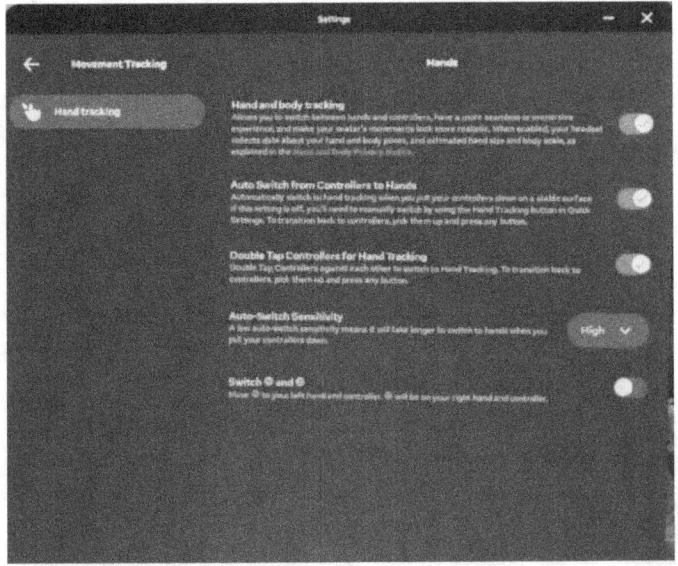

accessibility

On a phone, accessibility might not be a section you use very often; on the Quest, you may find it more helpful. Because of the nature of the device, you mind find things in this section useful.

Vision

The first area lets you adjust the contrast, color correct, and text size of the Quest.

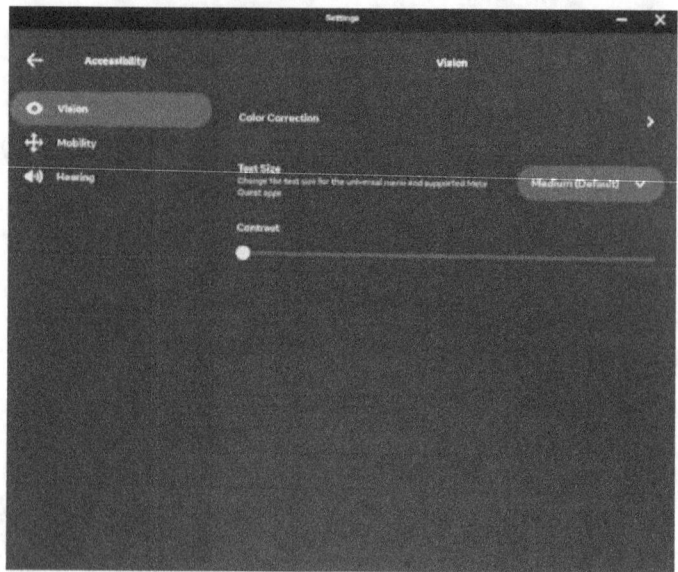

Mobility

Don't like the controllers vibrating? Or is it perhaps too strong? You can change it here.

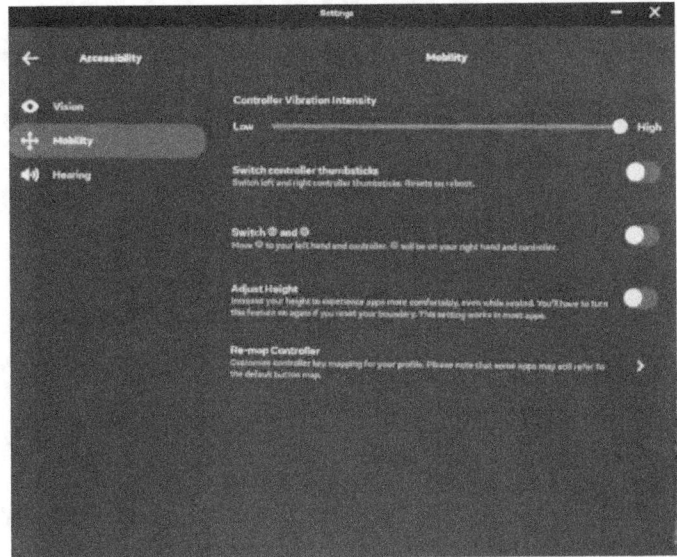

Hearing

And finally hearing is where you go to turn on Mono sound or, my favorite, turn on captions.

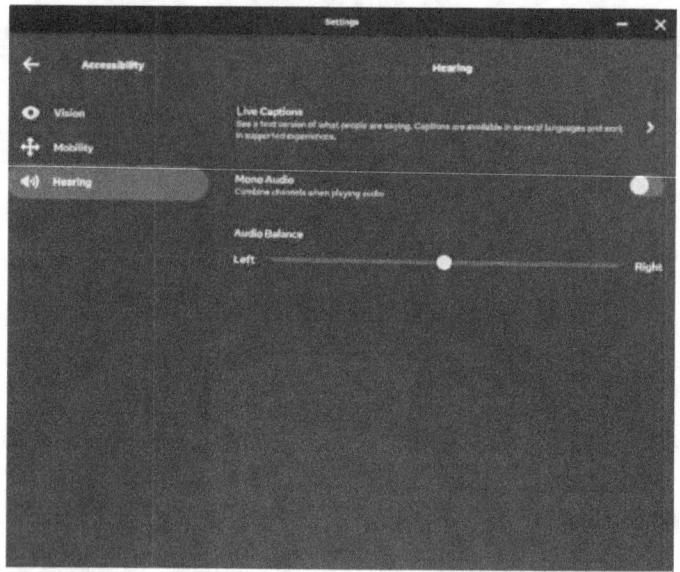

privacy

You've probably know all about Meta and their past troubles with privacy. They're trying to fix some of this past behavoior by making it easy for you to adjust what you share.

Audience and Visibility

Audience lets you pick who can see what your doing.

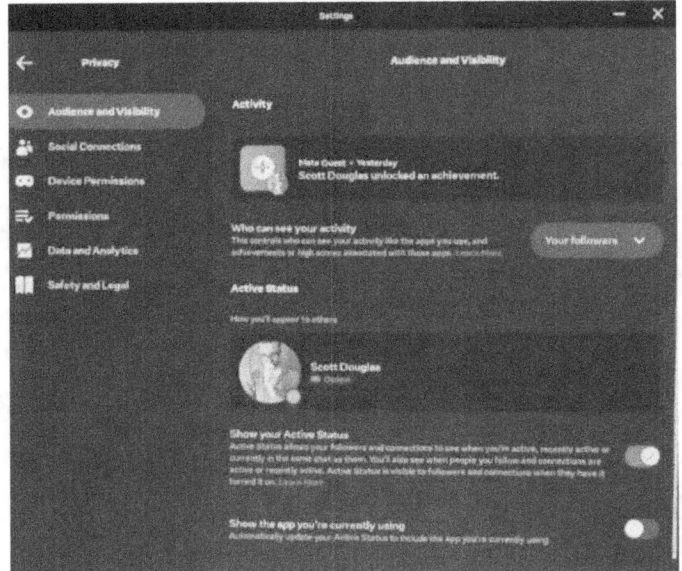

social connections

Social connections let's you add in different profiles and social accounts.

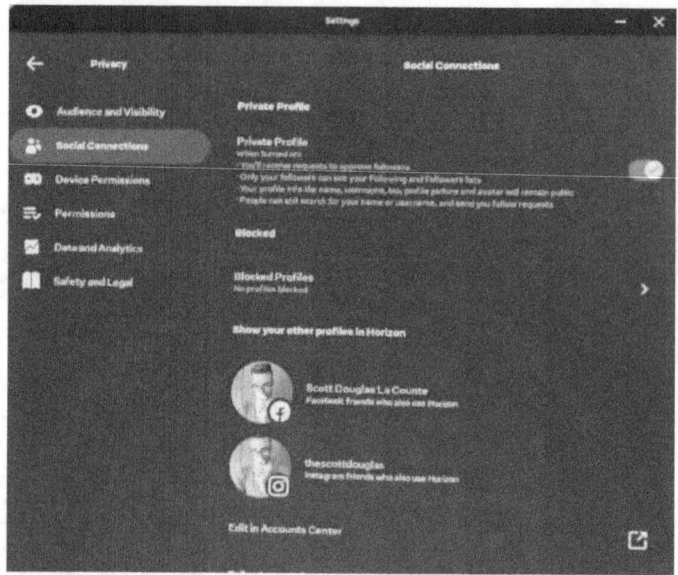

device permissions

Device permissions lets you turn on and off things like location services–meaning apps can see where you are located.

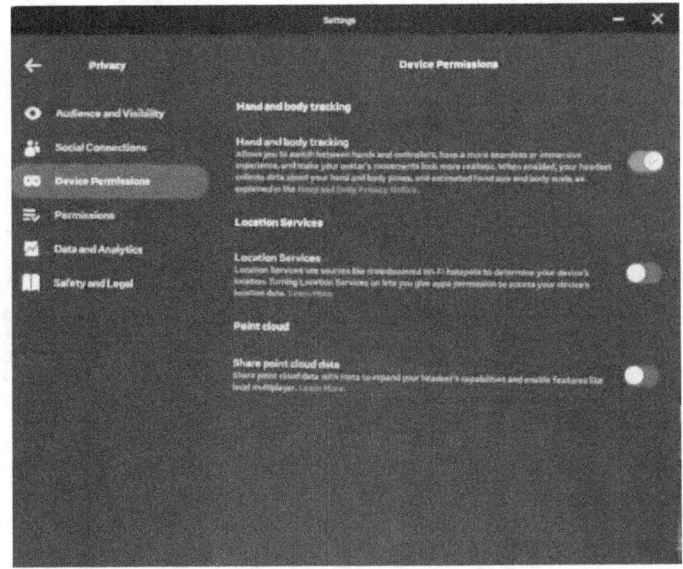

Permissions

Permissions will take you back to the Permission section of the settings. Why is it here as well? Your guess is as good as mine.

Data and Analytics

Data and Analytics is where your data is stored; it also lets you share it with developers to enhance apps.

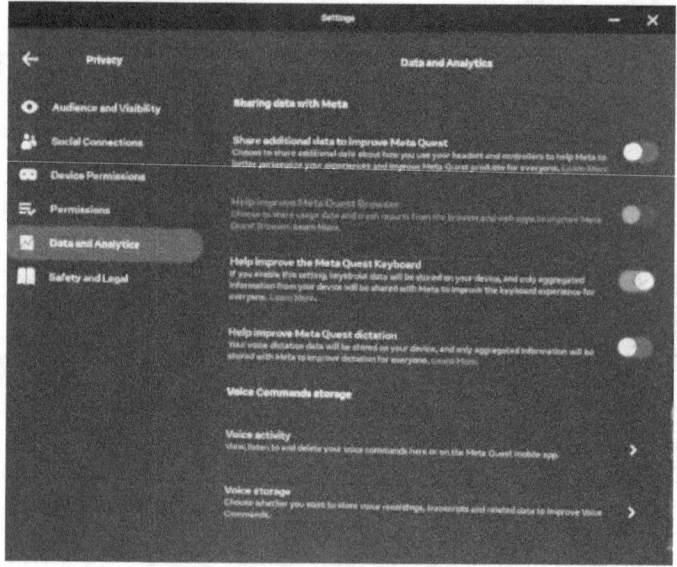

safety and legal

Finally the last option is just a link to all the terms and conditions. There's nothing to do in this section in terms of turning things on and off.

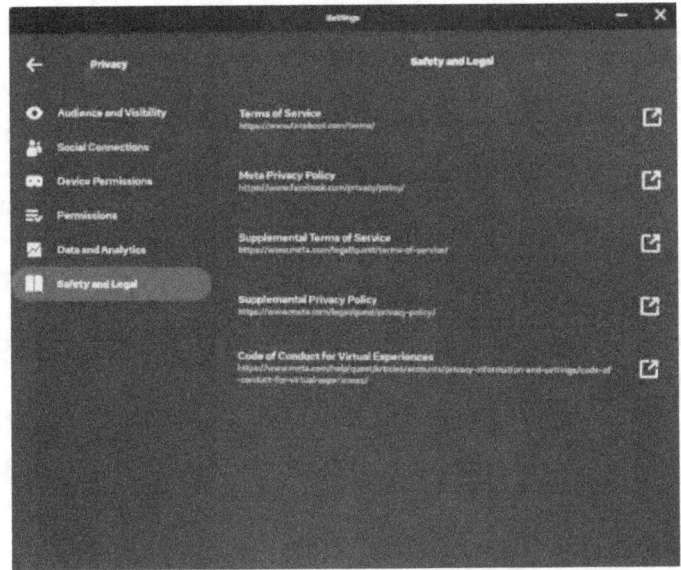

security

Do you have a lock on your phone or can anyone just pick it up and use it? You probably have a lock, right? What about your Quest? Do you mind if anyone picks it up and starts using it or do you prefer to have it somewhat locked down so people need permission to use it? That's what the security section is for. You can set up passcodes and turn on other features to make your device more secure.

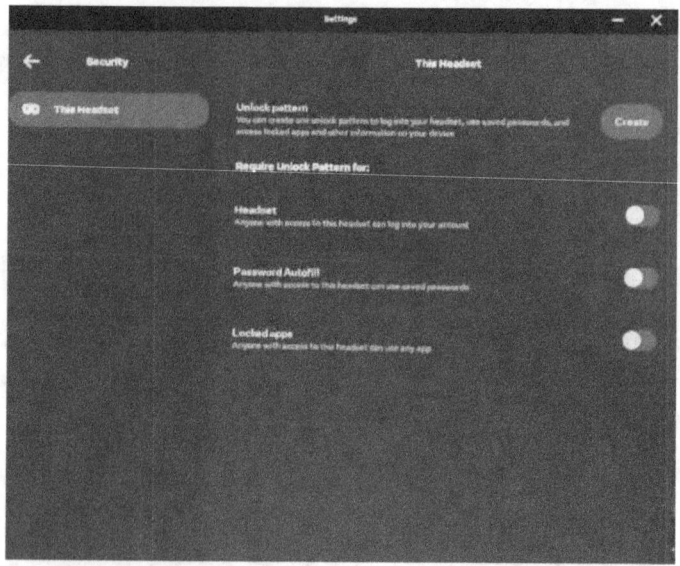

experimental

Occasionally there will be features to the Quest 3 that are still being tested. You'll find them here. They do work, but they might not work as expected.

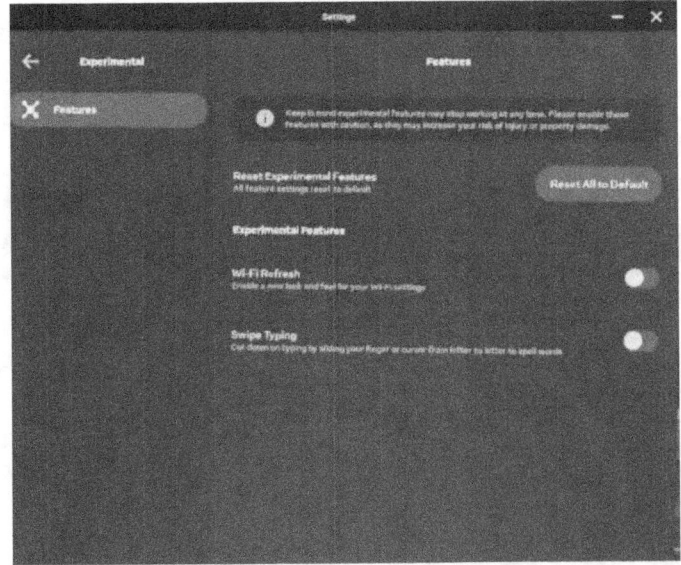

accounts center

This is where you go to manage the different accounts on your Quest 3.

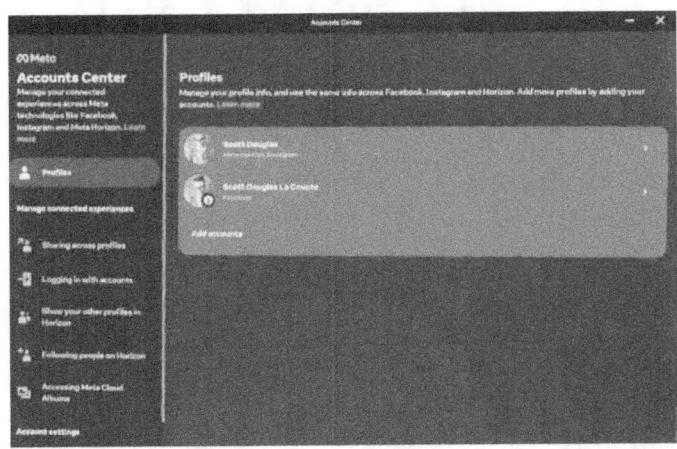

help

Help is where you'll find support articles.

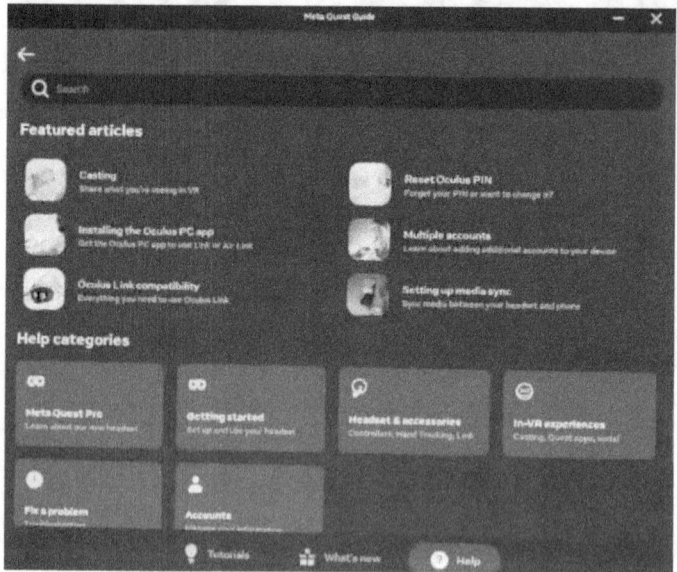

9 /
caring for your
quest 3

LIKE ANY TRUSTY TRAVEL COMPANION,
your headset needs a little TLC to keep it in tip-top
shape. Here's how you can show it some love:

Safeguarding Your Virtual Reality Companion:

- Shield from the Sun: Just like vampires
  and comic books, your headset has a
  nemesis: direct sunlight. Even a quick
  encounter with the sun's rays can hurt
  your device. So, keep it cool and shaded,
  and you'll avoid any sun-related
  mishaps.
- Avoid Sharp Objects: Think of your
  headset's lenses as its eyes to the virtual

world. Protect them from scratches by steering clear of pointy adversaries like cable tips or keys.

- Handle with Care: When you're fitting your headset, think of it as adjusting a baseball cap—be gentle and don't pull too hard on the straps.
- Power Safety: Charging time is nap time for your headset. Don't wear it while it's plugged in. This ensures both your safety and the device's longevity.
- Glasses Users, Rejoice!: If you're a specky VR explorer, use the glasses spacer included in the box for a comfortable journey into virtual realms.

Avoiding General Damage:

- Extreme Heat is a No-No: Just like chocolate, your headset doesn't fare well in high heat. Avoid leaving it in your car on a sunny day or near any cozy, but deceptively dangerous, heat sources.
- Pet and Toddler-Free Zone: Keep your device out of reach from curious paws

and tiny hands. They might love it a bit too much.

- Keep It Crumb-Free: Eating, drinking, or smoking near your headset could lead to messy accidents. Let's keep the party outside the VR space, shall we?
- A Secure Resting Place: When your headset's off-duty, store it somewhere safe—where accidents are less likely to happen. A drawer or a shelf can be its personal 'docking station'!

Keeping Your Gear Clean:

- Wipe Down After Each Use: A simple swipe with a dry microfiber cloth will keep your headset and controllers looking sharp. If you're the proud owner of a Meta Quest Pro, there's a special care cloth just for this job.
- Chemicals and Alcohol are VR Enemies: They might do wonders for cleaning your home, but keep them away from your headset. Stick to water if necessary, and use it sparingly.

- Lens Cleaning 101: Clean the lenses from the center in a gentle, circular motion heading outwards—it's like giving your headset a mini massage.
- Washables: The facial interface, elastic headstraps, headpads, and silicone covers can be wiped off for everyday dirt. If they need a deeper clean, remove them and hand wash with cool water and a mild liquid detergent. Make sure to rinse well and let them air dry completely before they're back on duty.

10 /
meta quest 3
accessories

THE META QUEST 3 comes with everything you need out of the box. But there are plent of add ons that you can buy depending on your needs. Let's take a look at them.

Meta Quest 3 Carrying Case: Think of it as your VR's home away from home. Protecting your gadgetry investments is crucial, especially if you're on the move. Plus, its sleek design and rounded profile aren't just practical; they're a style statement.

Meta Quest 3 Charging Dock: Imagine a world where charging is as simple as just placing your headset down. We're living in it! However, be mindful of your third-party accessories, as they might require some Tetris skills to fit snugly.

Meta Quest 3 Elite Strap: Ever had those

moments when, after a long VR session, you feel like you've had a mini workout? This strap aims to make your VR time as comfy as possible, distributing weight to avoid those dreaded pressure marks.

Meta Quest 3 Elite Strap with Battery: It's all the comfort of the Elite Strap with an extra jolt of energy. Perfect for extended VR adventures without worrying about running out of juice.

Meta Quest 3 Facial Interface & Head Strap: Stand out in the real world while you dive into the virtual one. Choices of Elemental Blue or Blood Orange not only give your device personality but also align with the latest color trends in the tech world.

Meta Quest 3 Silicone Facial Interface: Intense VR sessions can get sweaty. With this easy-to-clean silicone interface, you can keep things hygienic and maintain the plush comfort against your skin.

The Link Cable: This isn't just a cable; it's your gateway to a universe of incredible graphics and riveting gameplay. Make the most of your PC VR titles by bridging the gap between the two platforms.

Meta Quest Active Straps: VR mishaps can be both hilarious and catastrophic. These active straps ensure your controllers stay where they should - in your hands.

Zenni® VR Prescription Lenses For Meta Quest 3: Struggling with glasses in VR is now a thing of the past. These lenses offer a snug fit, ensuring you dive into virtual worlds with clarity and precision.

D-Link VR Air Bridge: If you thought your VR experience couldn't get any more immersive, think again. The D-Link VR Air Bridge promises enhanced gameplay, smoother graphics, and an overall upgraded experience.